T0323806

AI FOR COMMUNICATION

AI for Communication offers an engaging exploration into the diverse applications of artificial intelligence (AI) within the realm of communication. By bridging the gap between the scientific and engineering realms of AI and communication, this book reveals how AI, since its inception during the Dartmouth Summer workshop of 1956, has inherently been a science of communication. Exploring key advancements such as machine translation, natural language processing, large language models, computational creativity, and social robotics, this book shows how these innovations not only disrupt but also actively transform human communication.

The book is designed for students, teachers, and general readers who want to know how the field of communication impacts and influences the theory and practice of AI and how recent developments in AI will affect all aspects of human social interaction.

David J. Gunkel is professor of communication technology at Northern Illinois University (USA) and associate professor of applied ethics at Łazarski University (Poland). He is the author of 14 books on the social impact and significance of digital media, artificial intelligence, and robotics.

AI FOR EVERYTHING

Artificial intelligence (AI) is all around us. From driverless cars to game winning computers to fraud protection, AI is already involved in many aspects of life, and its impact will only continue to grow in future. Many of the world's most valuable companies are investing heavily in AI research and development, and not a day goes by without news of cutting-edge breakthroughs in AI and robotics.

The *AI for Everything* series explores the role of AI in contemporary life, from cars and aircraft to medicine, education, fashion and beyond. Concise and accessible, each book is written by an expert in the field and will bring the study and reality of AI to a broad readership including interested professionals, students, researchers, and lay readers.

AI for Sports
Chris Brady, Karl Tuyls, Shayegan Omidshafiei

AI for Learning
Carmel Kent & Benedict du Boulay

AI for the Sustainable Development Goals
Henrik Skaug Sætra

AI for School Teachers
Rose Luckin. Karine George & Mutlu Cukurova

AI for Healthcare Robotics
Eduard Fosch-Villaronga & Hadassah Drukarch

AI for Physics
Volker Knecht

AI for Diversity
Roger A. Søraa

AI for Finance
Edward P. K. Tsang

AI for Communication
David J. Gunkel

AI for Scientific Discovery
Janna Hastings

AI for Peace
Branka Panic
Paige Arthur

For more information about this series please visit:
www.routledge.com/AI-for-Everything/book-series/AIFE

AI FOR COMMUNICATION

DAVID J. GUNKEL

CRC Press
Taylor & Francis Group
Boca Raton London New York

CRC Press is an imprint of the
Taylor & Francis Group, an **informa** business

First edition published 2025
by CRC Press
2385 NW Executive Center Drive, Suite 320, Boca Raton FL 33431

and by CRC Press
4 Park Square, Milton Park, Abingdon, Oxon, OX14 4RN

CRC Press is an imprint of Taylor & Francis Group, LLC

© 2025 David J. Gunkel

ISBN: 978-1-032-58041-8 (hbk)
ISBN: 978-1-032-57170-6 (pbk)
ISBN: 978-1-003-44224-0 (ebk)

DOI: 10.1201/9781003442240

Typeset in Joanna
by Apex CoVantage, LLC

CONTENTS

Foreword   ix

1 Introduction: AI and Communication   1
   1.1 Communication for AI 2
        1.1.1 Interpersonal Communication 4
        1.1.2 Language 5
        1.1.3 Know Deception, Know AI 6
   1.2 AI for Communication 7
        1.2.1 Machine Translation 7
        1.2.2 Natural Language Processing 8
        1.2.3 Social Robots 8
        1.2.4 Large Language Models 9
        1.2.5 Computational Creativity and Generative AI 9
   1.3 Terminology 10
        1.3.1 Communication 10
        1.3.2 Artificial Intelligence 11
        1.3.3 GOFAI or Symbol Manipulation 12
        1.3.4 Artificial Neural Networks and Machine Learning 13
        1.3.5 Robot 15

2   Machine Translation   17
    2.1 Idea and History 18
    2.2 MT Methods and Approaches 19
         2.2.1 Classical MT 20
         2.2.2 Example-Based MT 22
         2.2.3 Statistical MT 23
         2.2.4 Machine Learning MT 26
    2.3 Consequences and Significance 29

3   Natural Language Processing   33
    3.1 Chatbots 34
         3.1.1 Chatbot Operations 34
         3.1.2 Chatbots and Communication 36
    3.2 Spoken Dialogue Systems 37
         3.2.1 SDS Implementations 38
         3.2.2 SDS Opportunities and Challenges 43
    3.3 NLP—Conclusions and Outcomes 46
         3.3.1 Communication 46
         3.3.2 Social Presence 47
         3.3.3 Deception 48

4   Social Robots   50
    4.1 The Rise of Social Robots 51
    4.2 Embodiment and Morphology 53
         4.2.1 Embodiment 53
         4.2.2 Morphology 56
    4.3 Opportunities and Challenges 59
         4.3.1 Anthropomorphism and the Uncanny Valley 59
         4.3.2 Real or Illusion 61
         4.3.3 Thing, Person, or Otherwise 63

5   Large Language Models   66
    5.1 Demystifying LLMs 66
         5.1.1 Language Model 67
         5.1.2 Transformer Architecture and Operations 69

5.2 Cost/Benefit Analysis 73

    5.2.1 LLM Benefits 73

    5.2.2 LLM Costs 74

5.3 Does Writing Have a Future? 79

    5.3.1 Death of the Author 79

    5.3.2 The Means of Meaning 80

    5.3.3 Words and Things 81

6   Computational Creativity and Generative AI   82

6.1 Automated Creativity 83

    6.1.1 Music 83

    6.1.2 Visual Art 86

6.2 Opportunities and Challenges 89

    6.2.1 Artworks and the Work of the Artist 89

    6.2.2 Original or Copy 91

    6.2.3 Deepfakes 93

    6.2.4 Responsibility 95

6.3 The Difference That Makes a Difference 96

7   The Future of Communication   98

7.1 AI Is the Future of Communication 98

    7.1.1 Communication and Technology 99

    7.1.2 Computer-Mediated Communication 100

    7.1.3 From CMC to AI-MC and HMC 101

7.2 Communication Is the Future of AI 103

    7.2.1 The Name Game 104

    7.2.2 Back to the Future 105

7.3 Opportunities and Challenges 107

    7.3.1 Responsibility 107

    7.3.2 Rights 110

References   115

FOREWORD

In a world teetering on the edge of the greatest technological revolution in history, Professor David J. Gunkel's *AI for Communication* emerges as a critical examination of the profound ways artificial intelligence (AI) is reshaping our understanding and practices of communication. This forward-thinking book invites readers into a dialogue not just about the changes AI is bringing to the field of communication but also about a fundamental reevaluation of who or what can be considered a communicative subject in the first place.

Professor Gunkel, with his extensive background in communication and technology studies, steers us through the complexities of this disruption with clarity and profound insight. The book delves into the nuances of human–AI interaction, questioning the long-standing boundaries that have defined communicators and recipients, senders and receivers, and creators and audiences. In doing so, Gunkel does not merely describe a changing landscape; he challenges us to reconsider our very notions of communication in an AI-infused world.

AI for Communication is not just timely; it is necessary. As AI technologies become increasingly sophisticated, they are not only augmenting human communication but also creating new forms of communication among themselves, with nature, and with the broader environment. Through a series of meticulously researched chapters, Gunkel illustrates how these advancements compel us to broaden our perspective on communicative agency, moving beyond anthropocentric views to embrace a more inclusive, interaction-based understanding.

This book serves as a beacon for students, scholars, professionals, and anyone interested in the intersections of communication, technology, and society. Gunkel's exploration goes beyond academic discourse, touching on ethical, philosophical, and practical questions that affect us all. How do we define the rights of a communicative subject that is not human? What responsibilities do developers and users of AI technologies have in this new communicative ecosystem? How do we navigate the challenges of privacy, consent, and agency?

In *AI for Communication*, Professor David J. Gunkel not only provides the framework for addressing these questions but also inspires a sense of responsibility and curiosity in the reader. As we stand at the precipice of this new era, Gunkel's work is a vital compass, guiding us through uncharted territories with wisdom and foresight. This book is an invitation to participate in shaping a future where communication is not just about transmitting information but about fostering connections that respect and honor all forms of communicative life.

Welcome to a journey that redefines the essence of communication in the age of artificial intelligence. Welcome to *AI for Communication*.

1

INTRODUCTION

AI AND COMMUNICATION

This book connects the dots between artificial intelligence (AI) and communication. It identifies and investigates the different ways that advancements in the field of AI—specifically machine translation (MT), natural language processing (NLP), large language models (LLMs), social robots, and computational creativity—disrupt and are in the process of transforming human communication as we have known it. The book is designed for students, teachers, and general readers who want to know how the field of communication intersects with AI and how recent developments in the techniques and technology of AI will affect all aspects of human social interaction.

But if you read the Foreword, you already know all this. In fact, the Foreword does a rather good job—maybe even a better job—of describing what this book is about and why it is important. I cannot, however, take credit for that. The Foreword was not written by me. It was not even written by another human being. It was generated by prompting a large language model, specifically OpenAI's ChatGPT, with the following:

> Write a brief foreword to a book by Professor David J. Gunkel and titled *AI for Communication*. The book describes the various

DOI: 10.1201/9781003442240-1

ways that AI is disrupting communication by asking us to rethink who or what can be a communicative subject.

What is significant about the Foreword, then, is not just what is communicated in the words of that text but also how it came to be written. Unlike the word processing application that I am using right now, ChatGPT was not a tool or instrument that I employed to compose the Foreword. The Foreword was composed by the AI. But in that case, how are we to read and make sense of this kind of machine-generated content? Typically, a written text is understood to be the product of an author who has something to say. So, if we proceed by asking the usual questions—"who is it that is speaking to us through the Foreword?" and "what do they want to communicate?"—those questions are not only difficult to answer but may even be meaningless insofar as there is no one, no human someone, at least, who is responsible for the words that appear on the page. But does that mean, then, that the Foreword is meaningless or has nothing to communicate? These are the questions of *AI for communication*. And they are questions that penetrate to the very essence of what we believe communication is all about.

This first chapter is designed to get things started. It will (1) demonstrate how human communication has, from the very beginning, been one of the defining conditions of machine intelligence, (2) provide an overview of the kinds of AI technologies and implementations that are disrupting communication and that will be dealt with in subsequent chapters, and (3) define some of the more complicated but important terminology that will be used throughout the chapters of the book.

1.1 COMMUNICATION FOR AI

Communication—specifically human-level interpersonal communication—has been the defining condition of machine intelligence from the very beginning. This is immediately evident in the groundbreaking paper from English mathematician Alan

Turing—"Computing Machinery and Intelligence"—which he published in 1950. Turing (1999, 37) begins the essay by stating his desire to respond to the question "Can machines think?" But instead of answering the question directly with a yes or no answer, he immediately notes a problem with the question itself, and that problem has to do with language.

In order to respond to the question "Can machines think?" one would need to know what the words "machine" and "think" mean. To resolve this, one could, Turing argues, conduct an opinion poll or survey to find out how people tend to understand and use these words. But this would, as Turing concludes, get you no closer to an objective definition of either concept. So, Turing does what any good researcher would do in the face of such a dilemma, he changes the question. Instead of asking and responding to the initial query, Turing devises a rather clever method for testing if and when it would be reasonable to say that a machine is actually intelligent. Turing (1999) calls this "the imitation game."

The game—which we now routinely call the Turing Test—involves three individuals: a man, a woman, and an interrogator. The interrogator sits alone in one room and submits questions to the man and the woman who sit alone in other rooms. The objective of the game is for the interrogator to determine the gender of his two interlocutors solely on the basis of their answers to his questions. In other words, the imitation game was modeled on a kind of gender guessing game where the interrogator could not see the respondents and had to make decisions about gender identity based only on answers to questions. Obviously, Turing was well aware that the tone of voice could influence results, so he further stipulated that the questions and answers exchanged in writing or through some kind of technical mediation like text messaging.

Given this initial setup, Turing (1999, 38) then poses this modification: What would happen when a computer takes the place of either the man or the woman in this game of Q&A? In other words, Turing imagines a situation where the interrogator is now exchanging messages with a human being and a machine. And the new objective of the game is to see whether the interrogator is able to differentiate the real person from the machinic imitator. Or to put it another way, can the machine pass itself off as another human person in interpersonal conversational exchanges such that the interrogator cannot tell whether they are talking to another human person or a computerized chatbot. If or when this happens, Turing concludes, we will be justified in calling that machine intelligent. There are a number of things going on here, so let's break it down and take note of three important items.

1.1.1 INTERPERSONAL COMMUNICATION

Turing redefines the question concerning machine intelligence in terms of interpersonal communication. Thus, the imitation game, as Simone Natale (2021, 25) suggests in his book *Deceitful Media*, might just as well have been called the "communication game." There are good reasons for this, and it has to do with what philosophers, psychologists, and behavioral scientists routinely call "the problem of other minds." Here is how the neuro-philosopher Paul Churchland (1999, 67) famously characterized it:

> How does one determine whether something other than oneself—an alien creature, a sophisticated robot, a socially active computer, or even another human—is really a thinking, feeling, conscious being; rather than, for example, an unconscious automaton whose behavior arises from something other than genuine mental states?

We usually resolve this problem by looking to externally accessible behaviors that are commonly assumed to be signs or symptoms of intelligence. For Turing, and for many who follow his lead, intelligence is something that is neither easy to define nor able to be directly accessed and observed. It is, therefore, detected and decided on the basis of external behaviors that are considered to be indicators of intelligence, especially communication and human-level verbal conversation in particular. In other words, because intelligent thought is not directly observable, the best one can do is deal with something—like communicative interaction—that is assumed to be the product of intelligence and can be empirically observed, measured, and evaluated.

1.1.2 LANGUAGE

As you may have already noticed, Turing does not use the phrase "artificial intelligence." That is because at the time he was writing, this term did not yet exist. We get it from the American computer scientist John McCarthy and a proposal for a summer workshop that he and a few of his colleagues had organized at Dartmouth College in 1955/56. In the proposal, McCarthy does not so much define the term AI as he provides a list of behavioral capabilities that would characterize its achievement: "An attempt will be made to find how to make machines use language, form abstractions and concepts, solve kinds of problems now reserved for humans, and improve themselves" (McCarthy et al., 1955). Notice that the first item on the list is a communicative ability—language use.

Subsequent efforts to characterize AI follow this procedure. In The Source Book of AI, an important textbook on the subject that was published in the 1990s, the editor Roger Schank (following Turing's lead) began by admitting the difficulty of defining the term "intelligence" and then proceeds (following McCarthy) by providing a list of "features that we would expect an intelligent entity to have." And first on that list is communication: "An intelligent entity can be communicated with. We can't talk to rocks or tell trees what we want, no matter how hard we try" (Schank, 1990, 4). Communication—especially linguistic communication—is not just one feature of artificial intelligence. It is a necessary condition. If something can explain itself to us in language that we can understand, it is considered to be both intelligible and intelligent.

1.1.3 KNOW DECEPTION, KNOW AI

The imitation game plays with deception. The objective of the machine in the game is to imitate a human conversational agent in order to effectively trick the interrogator into thinking that they are talking to another person even though they are simply chatting up a chatbot. For Turing and for the science and engineering practice of AI, this form of deception is not the exception; it's the rule. But deception—especially in social interaction and communicative experience—is not necessarily a bad thing. When you sit down to watch a film, the actors in the drama are pretending to be someone they are not in an effort to present a story. Technically, this is a form of deception, but it is one to which we not only have consented but find rather enjoyable and entertaining.

In the field of AI, this difference has been identified by Robert Sokolowski in an essay that grapples not with the term "intelligence" (which had been Turing's and McCarthy's big thing) but the other part of AI—"artificial." Sokolowski (1988, 45) notes that the word "artificial" has different and seemingly incompatible meanings. It can be employed to mean "fake" as in artificial flowers. But the word can also be applied to an artifact that is not fake, as is the case with artificial light. The light that emanates from a light bulb is "artificial" in comparison to the natural light of the sun, but that does not mean that it is fake light. It really is light; it is actual illumination that is produced by another means.

The important question here is which sense of the word "artificial" applies when we use the phrase "artificial intelligence?" Is artificial intelligence "fake intelligence," such that AI applications and devices would be little more than a magician's trick, a kind of deceptive illusion? Or is artificial intelligence a form of real intelligence—the emulation or simulation of intelligence—produced by other means? Not surprisingly, this remains a debated issue and a hotly contested matter even within the field of AI.

1.2   AI FOR COMMUNICATION

Because communication is hardwired into the very idea of AI, it should be no surprise that innovations in the field have a direct impact on communication—not just our everyday understanding of the term but also the academic disciplines of communication as well as existing communication industries and professional practices. There is, for better or worse, no aspect of human communication and social interaction that escapes from or resides outside the influence and impact of AI. Because of this, we are going to need to be selective, when it comes to investigating this subject matter. For that reason, the chapters that follow focus on and investigate five areas where the disruptive influence of AI for communication is already having a noticeable impact.

1.2.1   MACHINE TRANSLATION

We will begin by looking at machine translation (MT). MT, as the name implies, is the use of computer applications to bridge the gap that separates human populations from each other due to differences in the languages we speak. If AI is characterized as doing something that we think is typically a behavior or activity that takes intelligence, then translation is a good poster child.

You intuitively know this from your own experience studying and learning a second language. Translating between your native language (let's say English) and the second language (let's say Spanish) takes considerable memory and cognitive effort. Programming digital computers to do the same has been assumed to be a job perfectly suited to AI. In fact, MT is one of the first applications of the technology. But in taking over the task of translating between human languages, these applications not only displace human workers—translators and interpreters—but compel us to ask important questions concerning the nature of human languages.

1.2.2 NATURAL LANGUAGE PROCESSING

With MT, the machine is still regarded as a mediator between human senders and receivers. Natural language processing (NLP), however, takes things one step further by disrupting this standard formulation and making AI a participant in communicative interaction by occupying the location of sender, receiver, or both. One of the first applications to achieve this was Joseph Weizenbaum's ELIZA, which he introduced in 1966. Since this time, there has been a steady increase in the capabilities of NLP applications, with chatbots and digital assistants, like Siri and Alexa, now talking and interacting with us both on- and off-line.

These systems are efficient and convenient, mainly because they provide a conversational interface that is easy to use. But they also raise fundamental questions about who or what communicates. When we are talking to ELIZA or Siri, who is it that we are talking to? Can we trust what these things say? Should I say "thank you" to Alexa? And might these human-to-machine interactions not only replace human-to-human communication but lead to a deskilling of our own social capabilities?

1.2.3 SOCIAL ROBOTS

With NLP we have things that talk. But talking is not the only way we communicate. When I say, "it's just great that machines can now use language," that statement can have at least two different and entirely opposite meanings, depending on the tone of voice, facial expression, and body language that accompany it. One way to accommodate this in communicative AI is to put the NPL application in a body. This is the *raison d'etre* of social robotics.

Whether these devices have a humanoid form or not, social robots are socially situated technologies that are able to communicate in a manner that is reasonably close to achieving what would be expected of another human individual. But as the channels of communication are expanded—from language use to things like morphology, social presence, facial expression, and a wide range of non-verbal behaviors—we see a remarkable increase in the technical and social complexity of these devices. For that reason, social robots also up the ante on both the social opportunities and challenges of these technologies.

1.2.4 LARGE LANGUAGE MODELS

The current state-of-the-art in NLP is the large language model (LLM). Unlike many of the chatbots or digital assistants with which we are already familiar, LLMs do not use language by following prescripted conversational behaviors. Instead, they leverage the power of pretrained transformers, a type of artificial neural network that is trained on massive amounts of human-generated textual content. As a result, LLMs can produce all kinds of written material of remarkable quality. But they can also hallucinate facts and figures that are not true or entirely accurate. This is because, LLMs do not understand the words they process and generate, at least not in the way that human beings understand understanding.

With LLMs, then, we immediately confront a number of questions: How do LLMs work with language? Can we trust the information that they provide? What is the future of writing and literacy when machines can do the work for us? Does writing have a future? And have human writers been automated out of a job?

1.2.5 COMPUTATIONAL CREATIVITY AND GENERATIVE AI

As technologies of various sorts and configurations encroach on human abilities with language and other modes of communication, the one remaining bulwark of human exceptionalism appears to be creativity and artistry. Unfortunately for us, this may no longer be the case as there are already technologies that can produce what appear to be creative work in all areas of human endeavor—writing original stories for publication, composing and performing original music, making unique and innovative scientific discoveries, and generating new works of art.

In the face of these machine-generated works, we come face-to-face with deeply important questions: Is what is generated by generative AI original and new, or is it derivative and a cheap imitation? Can machines even make art? And if so, what does that mean for us, especially for those of us looking to make a career in one of the creative fields involving content creation like art and design, journalism, web development, film/video, music, or communication?

1.3 TERMINOLOGY

In the process of explaining the contents of the book and tracing its trajectory, it has already been necessary to use a number of technical terms and acronyms. Doing so is unavoidable in any kind of communicative effort like this. But before we get into the details of the individual applications of AI for communication, it would be prudent to take a moment to define and/or characterize some of the more important terms that will be encountered throughout.

1.3.1 COMMUNICATION

Communication is one of those words that we all kind of know what it means up until someone actually asks us to define it. This is not uncommon, and the problem is something that has been highlighted by communication scholars, especially James Carey. In an essay published in 1989, Carey points out that if you look up the word "communication" in a dictionary, you'll find two competing definitions. One definition—what Carey (1989) calls "the transmission view of communication"—focuses on the process of message exchange. It is concerned, as Carey explains, with the transmission of information from a sender, who has something to say, to a receiver. This is the way that communication has been explained and conceptualized with the standard process model, which was initially formalized by Claude Shannon and Warren Weaver in *The Mathematical Theory of Communication* (1949).

The other definition—what Carey calls "the ritual view of communication"—capitalizes on the shared etymology of the words "communication," "community," and "common." Unlike the transmission view, which focuses on information and its movement from sender to receiver, the ritual view is concerned with the way that communicative actions comprise and maintain specific social organizations and traditions. As John Dewey (1916, 5), who Carey quotes directly, explains:

> There is more than a verbal tie between the words common, community, and communication. Humans live in a community by virtue of the things which they have in common; and communication is the way in which they come to possess things in common.

These two views, it is important to point out, are not different kinds of communication. They are two different ways to look at—or two different theoretical vantage points for interpreting and making sense of—the same communicative event or social phenomenon. Consequently, Carey is not interested in promoting one view over and against the other. He is interested in the conceptual tension between the two views and what they can reveal about communication, its operations, and its impact on human social structures. In what follows, we will be careful not only to identify this tension but to highlight the ways in which AI can contribute to or even diminish one or the other viewpoint. In analyzing AI for communication, we will remain attentive to the full range and complexity of what is called "communication."

1.3.2 ARTIFICIAL INTELLIGENCE

The term "artificial intelligence" first appeared and was used in the process of organizing a research workshop in 1956. But what this phrase actually designates was, from the very beginning, unsettled and a matter of debate. "Artificial intelligence," as Roger Schank

(1990, 3) explains, "is a subject that, due to the massive, often quite unintelligible, publicity that it gets, is nearly completely misunderstood by the people outside the field. Even AI's practitioners are somewhat confused with respect to what AI is really about." Consequently, if there is some uncertainty for us about the term, this is completely understandable. Not only is AI generally misunderstood by people outside the field, it is misunderstood and mixed-up by those within the field.

Although this might initially seem to be a deficiency or "bad thing," it does have an advantage, which was explicitly recognized in the AI 100 report:

> Curiously, the lack of a precise, universally accepted definition of AI probably has helped the field to grow, blossom, and advance at an ever-accelerating pace. Practitioners, researchers, and developers of AI are instead guided by a rough sense of direction and an imperative to "get on with it."
>
> (AI 100, 2016, 12)

Although somewhat counterintuitive, the argument is that a lack of precise definition has actually helped the field of AI develop by allowing for and tolerating widely different approaches and efforts.

1.3.3 GOFAI OR SYMBOL MANIPULATION

One of the approaches to developing what is called AI is symbol manipulation. This method is based on mathematical logic and proceeds from the hypothesis that intelligence consists in the manipulation of discrete symbols. This method dominated initial efforts in the field and for that reason is also called "good old-fashioned AI" or GOFAI.

In GOFAI, developers write explicit step-by-step instructions that transform input into desired output. The recipe for a cake, for example, is a kind of GOFAI algorithm. Using the written instructions, which are specified in an ordered sequence of operations, you can take input—flour, sugar, eggs, etc.—and transform that material into the desired output—a cake. The same is possible, for example, with language translation. You can write computer code that represents various logical steps that takes input in one language and outputs a word in another language.

Three things to note about this. First, the capacity of these systems is often dependent on the number of lines of coded instructions. Obviously, to get something that even approaches what is available with any of the commercially available MT systems (e.g., Google or Bing), we would need hundreds of thousands, if not millions, of lines of code. Second, the "intelligence" of these systems resides in the knowledge and experience of their developers. In other words, the programmers of these algorithms generally need to know everything about the task and be able to code these items in explicit instructions (symbols). Finally, if something goes wrong with the system, the developer can always go back into the coded instructions, find the source of the error, and fix the problem by rewriting that line.

Despite the fact that this approach is routinely called "good old fashioned," many contemporary AI applications use it. This is because GOFAI is particularly good for problems that require abstract reasoning, i.e., problems where developers can abstract a desired behavior or outcome into distinct steps that can be encoded and followed by a computer.

1.3.4 ARTIFICIAL NEURAL NETWORKS AND MACHINE LEARNING

Artificial neural networks (ANN) provide for a distinctly different way of developing AI. In this case, developers use a number of artificial neurons—basically a simple threshold logic device that is described in computer code—and then connect these individual neurons together to form a network where the output of one neuron—typically a fractional number like 0.87—supplies the input to the next neuron. These connections, which are also described

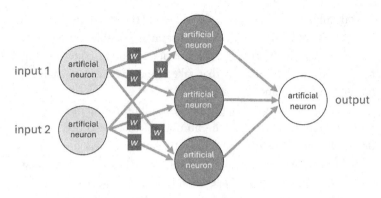

FIGURE 1.1 Diagram of a simple artificial neural network (ANN).

in coded language, are weighted with a variable multiplier (*w*) that increases or decreases the signal on that particular connection (Figure 1.1).

Data propagated through the network produce a pattern of activations in the interconnected artificial neurons that eventually results in some output. By progressively adjusting the weighed connections between the neurons in the network (a process that is called "backpropagation"), the system can be adjusted or "tuned" to exhibit different kinds of output behavior. This is called "machine learning." Consequently, the rules by which input is transformed into output are not specified as distinct (and static) logical steps applied to the input data. Instead, the network evolves the transformation procedures.

This approach to developing AI applications is better suited to situations that require extracting patterns from existing data. It works well when there is a lot of data about something, but developers do not necessarily know how to describe the desired behavior in an abstract form of step-by-step instructions. This means that the intelligence of an ANN does not reside in the developer; it is an emergent phenomenon. This does, however, produce two potential problems. First, an ANN is only as good as the data it is trained on. If you train the network with data that contains bias or other undesirable content, you can end up with an algorithm that spits out hate speech or other prejudicial content. Second, because the behavior of the ANN is an emergent property, developers often do not know what can go wrong with these systems until something goes wrong and then, because there are no explicit instructions in the network just weighted connections, it is difficult if not impossible to reverse things and correct the error.

While GOFAI dominated the field in the first several decades, ANN and machine learning have recently enjoyed a resurgence. In fact, all the attention—both the unrestrained hyperbole and the sky-is-falling alarms—that are currently associated with AI is largely due to recent innovations in machine learning systems.

1.3.5 ROBOT

Unlike the term "artificial intelligence," which is rooted in scientific research, "robot" is the product of fiction. The word "robot" came into the world by way of Karel Čapek's 1920 stage play, R.U.R. or *Rossum's Universal Robots* (Čapek, 2009), in order to name a class of artificial servants or laborers. In Czech, as in several other Slavic languages, the word *robota* denotes "servitude or forced labor." And since the time of Čapek's play, robots have invaded not only our science fiction but also social reality. Identifying what the word "robot" actually designates, however, turns out to be a bit complicated. In his book on the subject, *Robot Futures*, Illah Nourbakhsh (2013, xiv) explains it this way:

> Never ask a roboticist what a robot is. The answer changes too quickly. By the time researchers finish their most recent debate on what is and what isn't a robot, the frontier moves on as whole new interaction technologies are born.

One widely cited source of a general, operational definition comes from George Bekey's *Autonomous Robots*. "In this book," Bekey (2015, 2) writes, "we define a robot as a machine that senses, thinks, and acts. Thus, a robot must have sensors, processing ability that emulates some aspects of cognition, and actuators." This "sense, think, act" paradigm has considerable traction—evidenced by the very fact that it is called a *paradigm*. The definition, however, is broad and able to encompass a wide range of different kinds of technologies, artifacts, and devices. But it could be too broad insofar as it may be applied to all kinds of things that exceed the proper limits of what many consider to be a robot.

According to Bekey's characterization, the average thermostat could be considered a robot, as it senses a change in temperature, processes that information as being out of alignment with the desired result, and then acts by firing up the furnace. We could say the same of Siri. This application, which resides inside Apple's mobile devices, senses what the user says by way of the iPhone's microphone, figures out what the user wants, and then acts by conducting a quick Internet search and outputting this result in spoken language. Because of this, some roboticists have sought to further refine the "sense, think, act" characterization by adding one more feature: "embodiment." Robots, unlike digital assistants and cloud-distributed AI applications, have individual physical bodies that not only take up space but have social presence.

In the final analysis, we need to know that terminological precision, though maybe desired, is not going to be entirely possible. What one researcher calls "robot" another may call "AI." A lot depends on who tells the story, in what particular context, and to whom. In what follows, we will do our best to keep things clear and distinct. But doing so is already an uphill battle.

2

MACHINE TRANSLATION

Human communication is largely linguistic. Though language is not the only way that humans communicate, it is the principal mode of communication both in everyday understandings of the term and within the discipline of communication studies. But language brings with it one major complication, not everyone speaks or utilized the same language. There are, according to the most recent estimates, over 7,000 different languages in use across the world. And the consequence of this multiplicity is the subject of the Tower of Babel story, which is included in both the Jewish and Christian scriptures.

The way we typically resolve this problem is by translation, the process of transforming the expressions of one language into the words and phrases of another. Thus, a sentence like "Ludzie mówią różnymi językami" can be made accessible and understandable in another language, like English, by having the Polish sentence translated into "People speak different languages." For most of human history, this kind of transformation required the knowledge, skill, and experience of human translators, individuals who understood and could speak two or more languages. In this way, the translator was a kind of intelligent intermediary or medium who did more than simply convey the message selected by the sender to the receiver by transforming the message so that what was sent—a message

DOI: 10.1201/9781003442240-2

encoded in one language—could be transformed into another language that could be understood and processed by the receiver.

Today, this role—that of an intelligent intermediary—is increasingly being taken over and performed by artificial intelligence. This chapter will examine these MT applications. It will (1) briefly introduce the concept and recount its rather interesting origin story, (2) describe how these algorithms function by looking at different methods for developing MT applications, and (3) examine the opportunities and the challenges of MT for communication, especially what it means for language instruction and learning, international cooperation and interaction, and the future employment opportunities for human translators and interpreters.

2.1 IDEA AND HISTORY

The idea of MT begins with Warren Weaver shortly after the end of the Second World War. During the war, Weaver was head of the Applied Mathematics Panel at the US Office of Scientific Research and Development. In this capacity, he had the opportunity to experience the application of electronic calculating machines—what we now call "computers"—to the task of *cryptography*, the coding and decoding of secret messages. In 1949, Weaver, who had by that time returned to his pre-WWII position at the Rockefeller Foundation, wrote a short memorandum in which he proposed that translation between languages might be achieved by using the same tools. In fact, Weaver's memorandum introduced a number of important ideas that taken together frame the opportunity and challenge of MT.

First, the multiplicity of languages is a problem for international cooperation. "There is," Weaver (1949, 1) writes, "no need to do more than mention the obvious fact that a multiplicity of language impedes cultural interchange between the peoples of the earth, and is a serious deterrent to international understanding." So right at the beginning—in the first line of the memorandum—Weaver affirms and recognizes the communication problem that comes right out of the Tower of Babel story: linguistic difference is a significant barrier to intercultural exchange and an obstacle to mutual understanding and productive cooperation.

Second, there's a technological fix for this, and that fix is the computer. As Weaver explains:

> The present memorandum . . . contains some comments and suggestions bearing on the possibility of contributing at least something to the solution of the world-wide translation problem through the use of electronic computers of great capacity, flexibility, and speed.
>
> (Weaver, 1949, 1)

Though Weaver is optimistic about computer technology, he is also entirely realistic about things. He does not claim to have solved everything, but he is reasonably sure that the computer might provide a technological solution to the problem of linguistic difference.

Finally, the reason for this lies in Weaver's hypothesis that translation might be seen as a kind of cryptanalysis or code breaking. "One naturally wonders," Weaver wrote,

> if the problem of translation could conceivably be treated as a problem in cryptography. When I look at an article in Russian, I say "This is really written in English, but it has been coded in some strange symbols. I will now proceed to decode."
>
> (quoted in Poibeau, 2017, 53)

Whether Weaver's hypothesis is factually accurate or not is something that is still open to debate. What is not in question, however, is the idea of applying the experiences and tools of cryptography to the task of translation.

2.2 MT METHODS AND APPROACHES

The influence of Weaver's memorandum cannot be underestimated. The idea of overcoming linguistic differences by applying computer technology to translation definitely had traction. As a result,

Weaver's memo along with his access to lucrative funding opportunities in the US Federal government launched a concerted effort in MT that has, since that time, gone through a number of different technical phases or iterations.

2.2.1 CLASSICAL MT

Prior to the computer, translation efforts were supported by other technologies, specifically bilingual dictionaries, travel phrase books, and other kinds of parallel texts that present words or phrases in one language aligned with words or phrases from another language. If you have ever used one of these print resources, you know how this works. You scan through the list of words or phrases from the source language to locate the word or phrase you want translated. Since you do not know the language, this often involves matching sequences of letters and words, i.e., "Que hora es." Once you find the word or phrase you want translated, you will find it cross-referenced with the proper English phrase "What time is it?"

First generation computerized MT do pretty much the same thing, but they can perform the search and pattern matching much faster and more efficiently. In its most basic form, developers write a series of transformation rules that make direct associations between the words or phrases of one language and the words or phrases of another language. These coded instructions are just logical transformation steps, generally formulated as a sequence of if/then conditional statements. Here is what these steps would look like for a simple Spanish to English translation system:

    IF "Que hora es" RETURN "What time is it"
    IF "Buenos días" RETURN "Good morning"
    IF "Buenas noches" RETURN "Good night"

This short example demonstrates two important features of this approach. First, this method is not too terribly difficult. All you need is a series of coded instructions that transform the input of one language into the words and phrases of the other and then provide this as the output. Second, this approach to MT, like the bilingual dictionaries and phrase books that it emulates, is based on language pairs, like Spanish-English. Although rather efficient for two languages, these MT systems encounter problems as soon as one tries to scale this approach to accommodate multiple languages.

To see this, we just need to do a little MT math. For n-languages, you would need $n(n-1)$ translation models. So, for two languages, like Spanish and English, you would need $2(2-1)$ translation models, or one set of transformation rules for translating Spanish into English and another set of transformation rules to translate English into Spanish. If you have three languages $3(3-1)$, the number increases to 6. And if you want to accommodate nine different languages $9(9-1)$, you would need 72 sets of transformation rules. Thus, this approach can very quickly get out of hand and become difficult to implement and maintain.

One clever way to resolve this problem is to work with a third, intermediate language, or *interlingua*. This alternative systems architecture is more economical, requiring only $2n$ translation models. If we wanted, for instance, to design a system to translate between Spanish, French, and German, we could utilize English as an interlingua. This would require only six translation modules: three to translate the source languages into English and three to translate out of English into the target languages. The imposition of an interlingua, although clearly expedient for effectively managing the number of translation models, is not without linguistic and cultural consequences. By translating every language into and out of the interlingua, the translation system effectively privileges one particular language, restricting all possible expressions to concepts and logics that are germane to that particular idiom. Although this potential ethnocentrism is not necessarily a deal breaker for translation, it can lead to problems, especially when the mediating language belongs to a historically situated colonial power.

2.2.2 EXAMPLE-BASED MT

In the early 1980s, Makato Nagao recognized that classical, rule-based MT systems, which performed reasonably well for translations between different European languages, had considerable problems when applied to languages from different linguistic groups, like English and Japanese. To remedy this, Makato proposed a new kind of MT procedure that was based on how we actually work with language. Human beings, Makato argued, do not produce translations by following the kind of rule-based approaches operationalized in classical MT. Instead, they translate by following existing examples. Example-based MT, as this new method was called, simply seeks to develop algorithms that can achieve this kind of inference automatically by searching for and locating fragments of aligned translations in existing bilingual texts, extracting and storing these translated fragments, and then recombining the different fragments in order to produce more or less acceptable output in the target language.

An example might help. Imagine, as Thierry Poibeau (2017, 112) proposes, that we want to translate the English sentence "Training is not the solution to every problem" into French and that a set of bilingual texts is available with, among others, the following pairs of sentences (Table 2.1).

TABLE 2.1 Segment of a Bilingual Corpus for Translations between English and French

	ENGLISH	FRENCH
Ex 1	Training is not the solution to everything.	La formation n'est pas la solution universelle.
Ex 2	Training is not the solution to all parenting struggles.	La formation n'est pas la solution à tout les difficultés rencontrées par les parents.
Ex 3	There is a solution to every problem.	Il y a une solution à tous les problèmes.
Ex 4	There is a spiritual solution to every problem.	Il y a une solution spirituelle à tous les problèmes.

The translation system performs a simple text search (similar to what you would do when using the search feature in MS Word or other application), trying to match segments from the input text—"Training is not the solution to every problem"—to what is available in the bilingual corpus. In the process, the search identifies two matches for the phrase "Training is not the solution," which is associated with the French phrase "La formation n'est pas la solution," and two matches for the phrase ". . . to every problem," which is aligned with the French ". . . à tous les problems." By extracting and recombining (or more accurately stated "concatenating") these two fragments—"La formation n'est pas la solution" + "à tous les problems"—the system can then produce a translation of the English sentence, outputting the French: "La formation n'est pas la solution à tous les problems."

Example-based MT garnered considerable attention during the 1980s and was especially attractive for systems designed to handle Asian languages, which do not exhibit the same kind of linguistic similarities that are often available with Western/European language groups, like Italian, Portuguese, and Spanish. But this approach to developing MT applications does have important restrictions. For one thing, it requires a large number of parallel texts that are aligned, if at all possible, at the sentence level. Fortunately, this kind of data became increasingly accessible throughout the 1980s as documents were digitized and uploaded to the Internet. But even though the number of these parallel texts has increased since the privatization of the Internet, there are still situations where aligned fragments cannot be identified. When this occurs, example-based MT systems either fail or need to fall back on direct word-for-word transformations. As a result of this, example-based MT quickly gave way to and came to be incorporated into another technological innovation—statistical MT.

2.2.3 STATISTICAL MT

Statistical MT is based on and exploits the statistical nature of human language. The word order of a reasonably valid sentence in any natural language can be statistically analyzed and evaluated.

Consider the following words listed here in an alphabetical order: book, English, in, is, language, the, this, written. Some arrangements (sequential orderings of these words) have a high probability of actually occurring in everyday use of the language.

For example, this sequence of words would have a rather high probability of actually occurring: "This book is written in the English language." However, other sequences of the same words would have a very low probability, e.g., "Book language the is English this in written." Additionally, there are sequences of Portuguese words—"Este livro está escrito em inglês"—that would have a higher probability of being recognized as a valid translation of the English sentence than some other sequences of Portuguese words, like "Em está inglês livro este escrito." Statistical MT simply utilizes this observed fact regarding human languages to produce mechanized translation procedures.

Here's how it works. Let's say we want to translate the following Spanish sentence into English: "Quiero ir a la playa más bonita." We begin by dividing this sentence into verbal chunks, either individual words or short sequences of closely associated words: Quiero | ir | a | la playa | más bonita. We then consult a set of bilingual texts to find all the different ways human translators have translated these words (or sequence of words) in the past. For a translation algorithm running on a digital computer, the Internet is an obvious source for this kind of data. This produces a bilingual dictionary with each word from Spanish associated with its possible English translations along with a statistical ranking that indicates the probability for that particular correlation (Table 2.2).

From this data the algorithm can then generate 1000s of different possible translations, basically different arrangements of words in English that have a high likelihood of being valid translations of the source text. It then evaluates these different possible word sequences by consulting a statistical language model for the target language, meaning it evaluates the probability that one or more of the generated sentences have, in fact, actually occurred in English.

TABLE 2.2 A List of Possible English Translations for the Individual Verbal Units in the Source Language and Their Associated Probabilities as Discovered in Data Available from Existing Examples

QUIERO	IR	A	LA PLAYA	MÁS BONITA
I want 0.33	to go 0.31	to 0.44	the beach	more pretty 0.33
I love 0.26	to work 0.14	at 0.31	0.55	most pretty 0.18
I like 0.18	to run 0.22	per 0.25	the seaside	more lovely 0.32
I try 0.15	to be 0.05		0.45	most lovely 0.17
I mean 0.08	to leave 0.28			

TABLE 2.3 Possible English Sentences and the Probability of Actually Occurring in Existing Texts or Corpora

I love	to be	at	the seaside	most lovely	0.39
I like	to leave	per	the beach	more pretty	0.05
I mean	to be	at	the seaside	more lovely	0.11
I want	to go	to	the beach	most lovely	0.45

In other words, of all the sentences that are generated, some will be more likely to occur than others. So the algorithm simply identifies the one or ones that are most likely to occur and then disregards the rest (Table 2.3).

Looking at the probabilities available in this example, it is clear that the final sentence, which has a probability of 0.45, is the most likely candidate for translating the Spanish sentence. So that is provided as the translation. Note that in this process the algorithm does not need to "understand" (and, in fact, cannot "understand") what is meant by the Spanish sentence or its English equivalent. It is only arranging and evaluating different sequences of words or verbal tokens. It performs the task of translation for us by identifying the most probable associations between different sequences of words as exemplified in the existing parallel texts to which it has access.

The major advantage of statistical MT is that it is able to leverage the best of both worlds. Like example-based MT, it calls upon and utilizes the numerous examples that are available in machine readable parallel texts, basically calling upon and remixing decades of translation experience from human translators. At the same time, it is also able to capitalize on what made classical MT attractive in the first place—the ability to work with individual words or very small verbal units, thus producing a more robust translation system. For this reason, statistical MT quickly took over the field around the turn of the century.

Despite its success, however, statistical MT is not without its problems. First, the quality of translation is limited by the parallel texts to which the system has access, and this is, as you might anticipate, not evenly distributed. Some language pairs, like English and French, are well represented. Others, like Icelandic and Cambodian, are not. This introduces a kind of systemic bias, where some language pairs will have much better translation capabilities than others. Second, because of the extensive coding necessary to build and maintain these various statistical models, this approach to MT is labor intensive and expensive. Keeping a statistical MT system up-to-date and operational required an army of human coders.

2.2.4 MACHINE LEARNING MT

Because of these problems, statistical MT eventually gave way to machine learning approaches. The basic idea for this fourth methodology was introduced in a scientific paper from 2014 written by a team of Canadian and European researchers under the direction of Kyunghyun Cho (2014). The paper was titled "Learning Phrase Representations using RNN Encoder–Decoder for Statistical Machine Translation," and it is the combination of these two innovations—recurrent neural networks (RNN) and encoding/decoding—that makes everything possible.

An RNN is a neural network where the previous state of the network is used as one of the inputs to the next calculation, allowing the network to discover patterns in a sequence of data. Because human languages are little more than a set of complex patterns (sequences of different arrangements of a finite set of elements), RNNs can be used to "learn"—or perhaps better stated "discover" or "identify"—patterns that exist within and comprise a particular language.

Encoding is the process of making numerical measurements of input data. This is accomplished by feeding the RNN each word in a sentence one after the other until all words in the sentences have been processed. Because the RNN incorporates the results of previous calculations into the next operation, the final encoding represents all the words in the sentence. Or as Poibeau (2017, 185) explains, "Each word is encoded through a vector of numbers and all the word vectors are gradually combined to provide a [numeric] representation of the whole sentence."

We can now create a translation system by connecting two RNNs in a configuration that is called "sequence-to-sequence." In this "Seq2Seq" model, the first RNN generates an encoding that represents a particular sentence. The second RNN can then take the encoded data (the output of the first RNN) and perform the same operation in reverse order, decoding the numerical data in order to reproduce the initial input sentence. Obviously, this procedure, i.e., encoding and then decoding the initial sentence, is not very interesting or useful. But we can do the same thing using another language, like Spanish. In other words, we can train the second RNN to decode the fixed length vector representation of the sentence not into the original English but into a valid sequence of Spanish words by calling upon the associations that are available in a set of parallel corpora as was done in statistical MT (Figure 2.1).

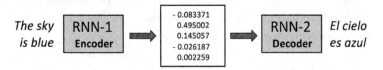

FIGURE 2.1 Schematic diagram of sequence-to-sequence RNN for MT.

Applying neural networks to the task of MT has a number of advantages. First, it tends to be more accurate and reliable. Because neural network MT is designed to encode and work with entire sentences without having to decompose it into smaller segments, it is able to preserve and account for context and word nuance. These systems can, for example, differentiate between the different meanings of a word like "bank," which can vary due to context—"I am going to the *bank* to get a loan" vs. "I sat on the *bank* and gazed across the river."

Second, these systems tend to be more efficient and less costly to develop and maintain. This is because the translation model is something that is automatically generated by the algorithm from patterns that are discovered in the training data and is not something that is dependent on the knowledge, expertise, and programming effort of human developers. Obviously human beings are still needed to design the network and set up its training on data, but the actual "rules" or instructions by which the translation takes place do not need to be defined and/or programmed. The machine is able to discover these things "for itself."

Finally, applying neural networks to MT has, at least in the short run, produced remarkable improvements in translation quality in a relatively short span of time. Even though this approach to MT is rather young—with Google Translate having just implemented it in 2016—it is performing as well as, if not better than, the statistical MT systems that took close to 15 years to develop.

This is not to say that neural network MT is perfect, and there are three important limitations and potential problems. First, like many machine learning applications, these algorithms can be criticized for being a "black box"—complex systems with internal operations that are not readily available to human oversight or understanding. In effect, we have translation systems that work, but exactly how they work remains a bit obscure.

Second, these applications need a massive amount of data. Like statistical MT, this approach utilizes the translation information provided by parallel corpora, meaning that translation is dependent on both the quantity and quality of these data. In some cases, there are a number of high-quality parallel texts to work with. In other cases, there are considerably less that are available in machine readable form. Consequently, like the statistical MT systems before it, neural network MT needs big data, and the larger and more robust these data sets are, the better.

Finally, big data means more resources to support data handling and processing. Working with large data sets requires Internet-connected servers that run on electricity and generate heat. Providing for this means that this approach to MT has material costs and that the impact of these technologies on the environment needs to be factored into their operations and expansion. Like other forms of neural network machine learning that are trained on big data, this approach to MT does have sustainability issues.

2.3   CONSEQUENCES AND SIGNIFICANCE

Clearly MT has come a long way. And it is definitely one of the most widely used applications of AI technology. It is readily accessible to users of the Internet through the web-distributed systems of Google and Bing translate. It is incorporated into many of our social media platforms. And it has been used for automated closed-captioning translation with popular online meeting applications like Zoom.

So, we can, at this point in time, return to where it all began and ask whether Weaver's prediction from 1949 was correct and accurate. Have we, in fact, devised a workable solution to the worldwide translation problem through the use of electronic computers of great capacity, flexibility, and speed? Or to put it more directly and in a way that matters for users of this technology, does MT make learning a foreign language obsolete? And do these AI technologies now mean that bilingualism is a meaningless skill and that human translators are now being automated out of a job? Interestingly the answer to these questions must be both "yes" and "no." It all depends on how we understand language, linguistic difference, and communication.

If communication is understood as little more than a means of message transmission, and if linguistic difference is understood as an obstacle to this transaction, then MT seem to promise a solution that is on par with or at least very close to achieving what has been imagined in science fiction with *Star Trek's* Universal Translator or the Babel Fish from the *Hitchhiker's Guide to the Galaxy*. You can, right now, travel the world and, by way of a smartphone app, simply point the phone's camera at some text, e.g., a sign or restaurant menu, and have Google Translate immediately render the unfamiliar words and phrases in your native language. And by employing some augmented reality (AR) visualization techniques, the scene you see on the phone's screen can look exactly like the world outside with one exception, the text that is displayed is rendered in another language of your choosing.

Similarly by using Microsoft's Skype Translator, you can seamlessly interact with another person, who speaks an entirely different language, in real-time over the Internet. In other words, a person in Australia who only speaks English can have an intelligible conversation with someone in Germany who only speaks Deutsch. The application renders spoken English into understandable German and vice versa, thus mediating the linguistic difference between the two participants. Consequently, and looked at from this vantage point, it appears that these MT applications and tools do in fact bridge the divide and call for an end or at least a significant reevaluation of the need to learn other languages.

But not so fast. There is more to it, a lot more. Language is not just a tool of information transmission. It is also, as James Carey (1989) pointed out, the common experience and carrier of culture. In other words, languages are not just different ways of encoding thought, as Weaver had assumed in his "Translation" memo. They are also the shared means of thought such that different languages make available different ways of thinking about and engaging with the world. The proverbial illustration of this (something initially reported by the anthropologist Franz Boas and repeated with considerable regularity in both the academic and popular literature) is that the Inuit languages of the Arctic contains many different names for what we, in English, call "snow," each one identifying a different aspect of the phenomenon not necessarily accessible to or able to be captured by the others.

Considered from this perspective, linguistic diversity might not be a bug that needs to be fixed; it might, in fact, be a feature. Here is how George Steiner (1975, 233) explains it in his book-length examination of translation called *After Babel*:

> The ripened humanity of language, its indispensable conservative and creative force live in the extraordinary diversity of actual tongues, in the bewildering profusion and eccentricity (though there is no center) of their modes. The psychic need for particularity, for "inclusion" and invention is so intense that it has, during the whole of man's [SIC] history until very lately, outweighed the spectacular, obvious material advantages of mutual comprehension and linguistic unity. In that sense, the Babel myth is once again a case of symbolic inversion: [hu]mankind was not destroyed but on the contrary kept vital and creative by being scattered among tongues.

Steiner's reading advocates an inversion of the traditional interpretation of the Babelian narrative. He argues that the so-called "catastrophe" of Babel, namely the confusion instituted by the multiplicity of languages that had divided humanity, does not constitute a kind of damage to be repaired but is instead a substantial advantage. At Babel, humankind was not destroyed by confusion but was kept vital and creative through linguistic diversification. Like biodiversity, Steiner argues, linguistic diversity is a feature. It has ensured human ingenuity and survival.

If we look at language from this perspective, the learning of more than one language and the task of translating between different languages is not just about efficient and effective message transmission. It involves learning about, experiencing, and living-in a particular way of seeing, conceptualizing, and engaging the world.

What is interesting about MT, therefore, is that it can alleviate language learning of the assumption and burden of mere communication (understood as the transmission of information), opening up opportunities to see other ways to think about and work with languages. So instead of replacing language learning, the foreign language requirement, and the task of human translation, it is more likely that MT will have the effect of recontextualizing and reformulating the *raison d'etre* for studying and learning languages in the first place. Consequently, MT AI is not the end of the story; it is the beginning of a new chapter for communication.

3

NATURAL LANGUAGE PROCESSING

Machine translation is one particular application of a much more comprehensive effort in AI that is called "natural language processing" (NLP). In fact, making machines that can communicate with human users in and by manipulating what is called "natural language" has been one of the objectives of AI from the very beginning. It was the first item on the list of proposed tasks to be addressed and accomplished by the Dartmouth conference of 1956. It comprised the defining condition and test case for "machine intelligence" in Alan Turing's agenda-setting paper from 1950, and it has been one of the principal features prototyped in science fiction with the HAL 9000 computer of 2001: *A Space Odyssey*, C3PO of the *Star Wars* franchise, and the Samantha OS from *Her*. For this reason, working with, processing, and reproducing natural human language content is not one application among others; it has been and remains one of the definitive applications of AI.

This chapter (1) investigates the concept, technological features, and historical development of NLP applications, beginning with the first chatbot ELIZA and proceeding through recent innovations with digital assistants and other spoken dialogue systems (SDS); (2) evaluates the opportunities and challenges of NLP in the context of communication; and (3) identifies and examines future social opportunities and challenges, where communicative interaction is not limited to human-to-human transactions but also involves

DOI: 10.1201/9781003442240-3

human-machine communication. The chapter, therefore, seeks to ask and respond to two related questions: Can NLP applications communicate? And how do answers to this question affect the future of human communication and social interaction?

3.1 CHATBOTS

When Alan Turing published his influential paper on machine intelligence in 1950, he had estimated that the tipping point—the point at which a computational mechanism would be able to successfully play the game of imitation—was at least half a century in the future. It didn't take that long. In 1966, a computer scientist at MIT named Joseph Weizenbaum demonstrated a simple NLP application that was able to converse with human users in such a way as to appear to be another intelligent agent. ELIZA, as the application was called, was the first chatbot.

3.1.1 CHATBOT OPERATIONS

ELIZA was a rather simple application. As Weizenbaum (1976, 188) explained, it consisted "mainly of general methods for analyzing sentences and sentence fragments, locating so-called key words in texts, assembling sentences from fragments, and so on." Here is a typical ELIZA exchange:

ELIZA: Hello, I am Eliza.
User: Hello, Eliza.
ELIZA: How are you today? What would you like to discuss?
User: I want to discuss chatbots.
ELIZA: What would it mean to you if you got to discuss chatbots?
User: Maybe I would understand how they work.
ELIZA: What is it you really want to know?
User: Are you a chatbot?
ELIZA: Why are you interested in whether or not I am a chatbot?

In terms of its programming instructions, ELIZA's conversational behavior is facilitated by what Weizenbaum called a set of decomposition and reassembly rules.

> A decomposition rule is a data structure that searches a text for specific patterns, and, if such patterns are found, decomposes the text into disjoint constituents. A reassembly rule is a specification for the construction of a new text by means of recombinations of old and possible addition of new constituents.
>
> (Weizenbaum, 1967, 475)

By cycling through these decomposition and reassembly rules, ELIZA is able to produce an exchange of statements that appears to be a conversation. And as Weizenbaum discovered in his own trials with the chatbot, many people were taken in by it and even insisted that ELIZA truly understood them.

Since ELIZA, there has been a steady evolution in chatbot capabilities. Many of these NLP applications, like Kenneth Colby's PERRY (1972), Michael Mauldin's CHATTERBOT (1994), and Richard Wallace's A.L.I.C.E. (1995), employed simple rule-based GOFAI architectures similar to what had been utilized by Weizenbaum. Later developments, like Rollo Carpenter's Cleverbot (1997), Steve Worswick's Kuki (2012), and Microsoft's Tay.ai (2016), moved beyond predefined scripted responses to corpus-based systems designed to mine existing human-to-human conversations or previous human-machine interactions. Today, chatbots have not only become reasonably capable conversational partners but can be found all over the place. They populate the virtual worlds of video and online computer games. They provide real-time online support and interactive help for most web applications and platforms. And they are now the first point of contact for most, if not all, customer service relationships and public-facing corporate communication.

3.1.2 CHATBOTS AND COMMUNICATION

When we evaluate these applications from the perspective of communication, all chatbots, irrespective of design, share three important characteristics.

1. Q&A Format—chatbot interaction is restricted to a narrow range of interpersonal behaviors. Following the initial stipulations of Turing's game of imitation, chatbots have typically been designed as question-and-answer systems. Either the user prompts the bot with a question and the bot responds. Or the bot begins by posing a question, like ELIZA's "What would you like to talk about?" and the human responds. Restricting communicative interaction to Q&A exchanges is a deliberate and rather artificial constraint that has the effect of limiting the range of conversational activity.

2. Text-Based Interaction—these Q&A responses are restricted to typewritten text. This limitation is not immaterial; it is actually a crucial design element that is advantageous to the operation of chatbots, especially on the Internet. By participating in text-based exchanges, a bot can easily be mistaken for and "pass" as another human user. In other words, chatbots capitalize on the technical exigency of online social interaction, where conversational engagement, whether between two human users or a human user and a bot, is limited to the circulation of typewritten statements. Consequently, all that is needed are the rudiments of some kind of perceived social presence in order for human users to mistakenly assume that they are talking to *someone* instead of *something*. Thus, the apparent intelligence of the bot is as much a product of bot's operations as it is a product of the tightly controlled social context in which the device operates.

3. Role-Playing—chatbots are designed to play the role of another human conversational agent, and their success (or lack thereof) depends upon how well (or how poorly) they

perform this task. One way that chatbot developers control for this is by deliberately designing the bot as a kind of character with a distinct personality. ELIZA, for instance, was intended to play the role of a Rogerian therapist. This not only explains the bot's manner of conversational interaction—basically turning user statements back on themselves—but also provides a predefined context that can constrain and control for what the bot can be expected to talk about. Another chatbot, Eugene Goostman, was designed to portray a 13-year-old Ukrainian boy. This characterization established expectations that helped users excuse the bot's limited conversational abilities, lack of general knowledge, and even grammatical mistakes that appeared in its output.

3.2 SPOKEN DIALOGUE SYSTEMS

Another widely accessible and popular application of NLP AI are spoken dialogue systems (SDS). These devices, which go by a number of different names—i.e., smart speaker, digital assistant, conversational user interface—are ostensibly chatbots that can process and produce human speech. Technically speaking, SDS applications, whether Apple's Siri, Amazon's Alexa, or Google's Assistant, are not one technology but consist of at least three different but related technological innovations: automatic speech recognition (ASR), dialogue management (DM), and text-to-speech (TTS) synthesis (Figure 3.1).

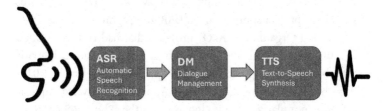

FIGURE 3.1 Spoken dialogue system (SDS) block diagram.

1. Automatic Speech Recognition—despite their technical advancements beyond simple text-based chatbots like ELIZA, SDS are still designed for and operate with text data. Consequently, the principal task of the ASR is to convert an acoustic speech signal to a sequence of discrete textual symbols (words) that can be processed by the computer.

2. Dialogue Management—The DM consists of two sub-systems: Natural Language Understanding (NLU) and Natural Language Generation (NLG). The NLU component parses the output of the ASR by analyzing the text string into its component parts and generating a semantic representation of what was said. The NLG then assembles a valid response that will be sent to the TTS for output to the user. In most contemporary SDS, this is accomplished by inserting information obtained from an Internet search into predefined sentence templates.

3. Text-to-Speech Synthesis—The task of the TTS module is to convert the textual output of the DM (or the NLG component of the DM) into an audible form that simulates intelligible speech. This is accomplished either through concatenation synthesis, which uses a library of prerecorded samples that are assembled piece-by-piece in order to produce a legible spoken message, or formant or articulatory synthesis, both of which produce the audio waveform algorithmically without relying on prerecorded samples.

3.2.1 SDS IMPLEMENTATIONS

Siri—One of the first commercially available SDS applications was Siri, a project spun-off from DARPA's Cognitive Assistant that Learns and Organizes (CALO) program that had run from 2003 to 2008. It was initially developed at SRI International, made available as a free app in the Apple App Store in February 2010, and shortly thereafter acquired by Apple. The software application was popularized via its inclusion in the iPhone 4S (initially released in 2011) and is currently an integral component of the

Apple iOS for smartphones and tablets. Technically speaking, Siri consists of four basic NLP innovations:

1. Speech Recognition—Siri employs an ASR engine, originally developed by Nuance Communication, which is capable of accepting and parsing spoken commands and inquiries in a number of languages. When you give Siri a command or ask it a question, your vocalizations are picked up by the device's microphone and recorded. Those data are immediately uploaded to the Apple server where they are scrubbed of background noise (an ongoing and persistent problem for any speech recognition system), statistically analyzed, and turned into text information that can be computationally processed. Siri's speech recognition engine is also designed with an on-device voice trigger and speaker recognition capability. When the device detects the wake-up phrase, "Hey Siri," it identifies the user and processes the rest of the utterance as a Siri request.

2. Natural Language Understanding—On the server, the resulting data are run through an algorithm that sifts through thousands of combinations of sentences to determine what the inputted phrase might mean. How Siri actually does this is a carefully guarded secret, but most contemporary NLU systems work by employing the same basic method. "A natural language system like Siri," as Macworld's Marco Tabini (2013) explains, "usually starts by attempting to parse the syntactical structure of a piece of text, extracting things like nouns, adjectives, and verbs, as well as the general intonation of the sentences." This later element helps determine whether the user input was a command to do something (i.e., send a text message) or a question (i.e., a request for information about current weather conditions). Fortunately, Siri does not need to "know" or "understand" everything that might be said

to it. The system is designed to operate within a rather narrow range of possibility and has been programmed to identify and work with those words and phrases that are required to fulfill tasks that it can perform. If the system receives user input that is not recognized as fitting this predetermined context, Siri is provided, like many of the chatbots before it, with a (sometimes sassy) pre-scripted reply.

3. Natural Language Generation—Once the NLU algorithm identifies the user's request, the system then begins to assess what task needs to be carried out. For Siri, which resides in a mobile device, this requires determining whether or not the information needed can be found in the device, i.e., play a song or access the phone's contact list, or whether it requires data from an online service. Once this has been determined, the application then formulates a response by inserting results into predefined templates.

4. Text-to-Speech Synthesis—Unlike a chatbot, Siri's responses need to be converted to audio data. This text-to-speech transformation relies on a library of prerecorded human voice samples—not whole words but individual phonemes, like the long "e" sound in the word "fourteen"—that can then be arranged in the correct order to supply audible output. This approach to concatenation synthesis requires hours of recorded vocalizations from human voice actors that are then isolated, catalogued in a database of sound samples, and reassembled into understandable audio content. The American English voice of Siri was originally performed by Susan Bennett in 2005, and Apple has tapped other voice talent to gather the necessary linguistic samples for the 22 languages that the Siri application currently supports.

Alexa—Amazon's voice assistant was initially patented in 2012 and released as a commercial product in 2014 along with the Echo smart speaker. Like Siri, Alexa is able to take vocal input, process this data, search for and obtain results, and then communicate this output to users in audio form. But unlike Siri, which has remained captive in the confines of Apple's proprietary systems and devices, Amazon has deliberately decided to make its cloud-based Alexa Voice Service (AVS) available to other manufacturers and device developers by publishing its API (application program interface) and offering developers a full SDK (software development kit) to aid efforts to integrate Alexa into their products. Amazon has even provided developers with tools to control Alexa's behaviors. One such tool, called Speech Synthesis Markup Language (SSML), allows programmers to control Alexa's pronunciation, intonation, timing, and emotional responses, customizing the way the application sounds.

Giving away its AVS for free might sound rather generous, but it is actually part of a rather savvy business strategy. Amazon wants to encourage and make it easy for developers to build the Amazon AVS into devices so that everything becomes a gateway to Amazon and its massive retail services. This capability, however, also points to one of the potential problems and pitfalls with using SDS devices and services. Since Alexa's "smarts" (like that of Siri) reside not in the device but in Amazon's cloud-based service, everything that is said to Alexa is recorded, processed, and stored on the server. When you talk to Alexa, you are also talking to Amazon.

Knowledge of this has sparked privacy concerns on the part of consumers. And there has been some negative press suggesting that Alexa could be "listening" and recording everything that happens in its presence. This criticism is not entirely accurate, as the device is only "listening" after being activated by a user employing the "wake-up" word, "Alexa." Until that happens, the device sits idle or in a state that could be called "sleep mode." But once it is activated, everything that is said to and in the presence of the Alexa-enabled device is recorded and stored in the Amazon cloud.

Google—Compared to its competitors, Google has been rather late in recognizing the importance of and responding to the need for SDS applications and appliances. In May of 2016, the company introduced both Google Home, a voice-activated smart speaker, and Google Assistant, a cloud-based virtual assistant. Like Siri, Google Assistant was initially restricted to Google devices and software (Pixel smartphones and the Android OS), but, following Amazon's lead, it has now opened Google Assistant to third parties so that the service can be integrated into all kinds of Internet-connected devices.

If Google was a bit late to market with its SDS products and services, it has recently taken a lead in developing more natural sounding conversational interactions with Duplex. Google Duplex (introduced in the spring of 2018) is an SDS application that is designed for completing specific tasks, such as scheduling appointments and obtaining information over the telephone. Google Duplex's conversations sound natural due to several innovations, mainly in the DM and TTS elements of the SDS. Duplex uses a recurrent neural network (RNN) built using the TensorFlow Extended (TFX) general-purpose machine learning platform. Duplex's RNN was trained on a corpus of anonymized phone conversation data, basically a large set of audio recordings and their written transcripts obtained from actual human-to-human telephone conversations—basically data from every telephone call that begins with the following statement: "This call may be recorded for training purposes."

Once trained, the network uses the output of Google's automatic speech recognition (ASR) technology in order to process and "understand" user input. One of the key features of Duplex is that it is designed to function within tightly controlled and constrained domains of knowledge, i.e., making restaurant reservations or scheduling an appointment for a haircut, and the "understanding model" was trained separately for each of these specific tasks.

In order to sound more natural, Duplex uses a combination of existing concatenative text-to-speech (TTS) with a new synthesis TTS engine constructed on Google's Tacotron and WaveNet technologies. To add to the realism of the vocalizations, Duplex is designed to model and incorporate speech disfluencies, those um's and uh's that are often utilized to signal that we are still processing or making sense of the conversational data. Because the spoken output of Duplex is virtually indistinguishable from that of a human being, Google has issued assurances that the system will always self-identity as an AI in order to avoid potential deception or confusion.

These three are a representative sample and not the only available SDS implementations on the market. There is also Microsoft's Cortana, which was named after an AI character in the *Halo* video game franchise and voiced by Jen Taylor; Samsung's S Voice and its successor Bixby, which is now being integrated in IoT (Internet of Things) home appliances as well as the company's mobile products; Amtrak's Julie, an interactive voice response agent for the company's automated information and reservation telephone system; and many others. Although the exact method of operation varies from system to system, the basic operations and components remain pretty much the same, such that the differences across these various SDS implementations are more variations on a theme as opposed to substantive differences in kind.

3.2.2 SDS OPPORTUNITIES AND CHALLENGES

1. Gender and Race—Though chatbots and SDS applications—like any technological object—do not have a gender or a race, they are inevitably gendered and racialized. ELIZA and Kuki have been gendered by their developers through the nominal operation of naming and by way of their character descriptions, and Kuki has been portrayed in her profile image (again something that was selected and created by her developer, Steve Worswick) as white. SDS applications add the additional component of vocal characteristics and speech patterns, which Turing had already identified as one of the principal signs of personal identity.

Siri's voice and behavioral characteristics were initially gendered female. This feminization of the device was not arbitrary. It was a deliberate design decision made by Siri's developers who sought to situate their SDS in the role of personal assistant, therefore occupying a subservient position that unfortunately mobilizes existing sexist stereotypes about gendered labor. Think for example of mid-20 century films where the secretary or office assistant is a spunky and flirtatious blonde, who not only organizes everything for her male boss but is always ready to help out. Subsequent distributions of the application have allowed for a wider range of voices, including a non-binary or neutral voice, that can now be selected by the user.

In addition to gender, the voices of most SDS applications have been criticized for "sounding white." As Miriam Sweeney (2020) reports, the vocal character of most of the commercially available SDS applications suggests a form of "'default whiteness' that is assumed of technologies (and users) unless otherwise indicated." Moving these decisions regarding the identity of chatbots and SDS applications to the user may be an improvement, but doing so does not necessarily escape the potential problems with stereotypes. It just repositions who is responsible for these decisions.

2. Anthropomorphism—Assigning gender or race to a computer application that does not possess either is a form of anthropomorphism, the attribution of human characteristics to inanimate objects and animals. On the one hand, this operation is both useful and seemingly unavoidable. Anthropomorphism is the way that we understand and make sense of another entity. We do not know what goes on in the head of another person or an animal for that matter, but in the face of these other things we often project into them intentional states, emotions, thoughts, etc. This is part of what it means to be social. In fact, we could say anthropomorphism is the social glue that

allows us to be social and to engage with others in meaningful interactions. SDS is no exception, and these systems not only encourage but also need anthropomorphic projection in order to function effectively as a socially interactive other.

But, and on the other hand, anthropomorphism has also been severely criticized as kind of wishful thinking that is out of alignment with scientific objectivity and rational decision-making. For this reason, many seemingly clear-thinking and level-headed individuals have argued that anthropomorphism should be curtailed or even eliminated altogether. The real problem here, however, is undecidability in the face of this human-all-too-human proclivity. In other words, we seem to be unable to decide whether anthropomorphism is a bug to be eliminated in order to expedite correct understanding and protect users from deception, whether it is a feature to be carefully cultivated so as to create better, socially interactive artifacts, or both. The fact is anthropomorphism happens. What we decide to do with this fact is what matters.

3. Corporate Exploitation—Most commercially available SDS applications participate in what Shoshana Zuboff (2019) has called "surveillance capitalism." When you talk to Siri or Alexa, for instance, you are not just talking to an individual device, you are also interacting with and providing personal information to Apple and Amazon, powerful multinational corporations that use this data for training their AI models and developing user profiles for targeted advertisements, recommendations, and prediction of consumer behavior. These digital voice assistants might appear to be affable and helpful companions, but this appearance often hides or veils the fact that they work for and are beholden to powerful and influential corporations.

Seeing through the persona or the mask of the SDS that is fabricated by both design choices made by developers and the seemingly unavoidable anthropomorphic projections contributed by users is not easy. But recognizing this fact is part and parcel of understanding the social role that these communicative technologies are designed to play, who controls and benefits from their deployment, and what benefits and risk users confront in the face of these artificial but very loquacious devices.

3.3 NLP—CONCLUSIONS AND OUTCOMES

NLP applications, like chatbots, SDS applications, and other forms of what have been called communicative AI, seem to have successfully achieved one of the stated goals of AI since the time of the Dartmouth summer research project—make machines use language. This achievement, however, has several consequences.

3.3.1 COMMUNICATION

NLP applications can use language, but is this communication? Answers to this question will obviously depend on how one defines and characterizes the term "communication." If we come at it by way of what James Carey (1989) calls the transmission view, it seems hard to deny that chatbots and SDS applications communicate. They are capable of receiving and processing user input, formulating responses by selecting messages, and then transferring those messages as output. The range of messages that these systems and devices are able to formulate may be limited, but these NLP applications are able to play the role of both receiver and sender in interpersonal conversational exchanges.

But chatbots and SDS can also play a social role in what Carey calls the ritual aspect of communication. A lot of what we do when we communicate is just circulate words with little or no attention to what is actually being said. We pass each other in the corridor and exchange pleasantries that are almost meaningless: "Hi, how's it going?" or "Hey, what's up?" In asking this, we do not really want the other person to respond with a long description of their current situation. In fact, doing so may even be seen as socially unacceptable. It's just a way of recognizing the presence of another as they pass you in the hallway. It is "small talk." But small talk, like this, is not meaningless. It a communicative performance that is necessary for creating and maintaining a common, shared experience.

These ritual practices are not about information that is sent from a sender to a receiver; they are about the routine operations that maintain communal or social connections. NLP applications not only can be designed to participate in this aspect of human communication, they are really good at it since doing so remains at the surface of the conversational exchange and typically does not require deep understanding of what has been said. These bots, in other words, are able to exchange words with us in ways that follow expected patterns of social behavior.

3.3.2 SOCIAL PRESENCE

Even if one is reasonably convinced that an NLP application, like ELIZA or Siri, is just a mindless instrument that merely manipulates linguistic tokens, experience with these systems shows us that it is how human users respond to these manipulations that make the difference. In other words, whether or not we conclude that an NLP application understands us or not, the communicative behavior that is exhibited does have an effect on us and our social relationships. This insight has been experimentally tested and confirmed by Byron Reeves and Clifford Nass's Computers Are Social Actors (CASA) studies, or what is also called the Media Equation.

The CASA model, which was developed in response to numerous experiments with human subjects, describes how users of computers, irrespective of the actual intelligence possessed (or not) by the machine, tend to respond to the technology as another socially aware and interactive subject. In other words, even when experienced users know quite well that they are engaged with using a machine, they make what Reeves and Nass (1996, 22) call the "conservative error" and tend to respond to it in ways that afford this other thing social standing on a par with another human individual. Consequently, in order for something to be recognized and treated as a social significant other, "it is not necessary," as Reeves and Nass (1996, 28) conclude, "to have artificial intelligence." All that is needed is that they appear to be close enough to encourage some kind of social response.

3.3.3 DECEPTION

But this "close enough" may have other consequences. Sherry Turkle (2011), an MIT social scientist specializing in the psychological aspects of emerging technology, worries that socially evocative technologies, like chatbots and SDS applications, are a potentially dangerous form of self-deception. In the face of apparently social interactive devices, Turkle argues, we seem to be willing, all too willing, to consider these technological objects to be another socially significant subject—not just a kind of surrogate pet but a close friend, personal confidant, and even paramour.

Consider, for instance, the experience of Robert Epstein, a Harvard University PhD and former editor of *Psychology Today*, who fell in love and had a four-month online "affair" with a chatbot (Epstein, 2007). This was possible not because the bot, which went by the name "Ivana," was intelligent in any sense of the word, but because the bot's conversational behaviors were close enough to encourage social responses. And this problem is not something that is unique to amorous interpersonal relationships. "The rise of social bots," as Andrea Peterson (2013, 1) accurately points out, "isn't just bad for love lives—it could have broader implications for our ability to trust the authenticity of nearly every interaction we have online." Case in point—national politics and democratic governance. In a study conducted during the 2016 US presidential campaign, Alessandro Bessi and Emilio Ferrara found that "the presence of social media bots can indeed negatively affect democratic political discussion rather than improving it, which in turn can potentially alter public opinion and endanger the integrity of the Presidential election" (2016, 1).

The challenge, then, is not just the potential for deception. It is also the undecidability that confronts us in the face of this very issue. Deception is obviously a problem and no one wants to be deceived, but it is also the defining condition of communicative AI and NLP applications since the time of Turing's imitation game. In an effort to sort this out, Simone Natale (2021) has suggested differentiating between "deliberate deception" and "banal deception," which he defines as a mundane and imperceptible form of illusion-making that operates by concealing the underlying functions of digital machines through a representation constructed at the level of the interface. The problem, then, is not that the potential for deception exists; the problem is that "deception" is not simply a binary. Like anthropomorphism, it can be both useful and dangerous. Thus, the real task moving forward is to learn how to manage these features in order to strike the right balance between benefits and harms.

4

SOCIAL ROBOTS

So far, all the AI applications we have considered involve language. And there's a good reason for this. Human communication is highly dependent on it. In fact, you might say that language is the defining condition of our species. But human communication involves more than language. Our spoken interactions are also accompanied by various forms of non-verbals, and, according to communication scholars, these are as important—and in some instances even more important—than the words that are spoken. One of the acknowledged limitations with the current crop of SDS applications, like Siri, Alexa, and the Google Assistant, is their inability to read, process, and reproduce non-verbal behaviors. And one way to address this is to put the AI in a physical body. This is the domain of robots and social robots in particular.

This chapter will (1) survey the development and uses of social robots, covering the range of current implementations; (2) examine the design and engineering challenges of creating different kinds of mechanisms with human-level interaction capabilities; and (3) evaluate the social opportunities and challenges of machines that are deliberately designed to occupy the place of another person or socially significant other. The questions that organize this chapter are: Can robots be genuinely social like another person or even a non-human animal? If so, how will this alter human social situations and interactions? And what will our world look like when robots live, work, and play alongside us?

DOI: 10.1201/9781003442240-4

4.1 THE RISE OF SOCIAL ROBOTS

Social robots are artifacts that are designed to interact with and respond to human users in a variety of ways and situations. Whether they have a human-form (like the androids created by David Hanson or Hiroshi Ishiguro) or not (like the Paro seal robot used in elder care or the Jibo robot developed by Cynthia Breazeal), social robots are technological objects that are able to interact and communicate in a manner that is reasonably close to achieving what would be expected of another social entity.

This can be achieved in different ways, and as a result "social robot" does not name one kind of device but encompasses a range of different kinds of implementations. Though there is some variation in terminology and nomenclature, most researchers recognize four different classifications:

1. Socially Evocative—These are technologies that are designed to facilitate and leverage the human tendency to anthropomorphize non-human things. Consequently, the social abilities of these robotic objects are actually a product of what the human user projects on and attributes to the device. Such robots do not need to be nor are they designed to be able to initiate, reciprocate, or even take part in the social exchange. A good example of this kind of social robot are robotic toys, like the Tomogotchis and other robotic "pets" that engage users' imaginations.

2. Social Interface—These robots are capable of exploiting human-like social cues and communication modalities in order to facilitate interaction with human users. Unlike socially evocative technologies, these devices require a sufficient level of "social intelligence" to perform meaningful communicative operations. But "because this class of robot tends to value social behavior only at the interface, the social model that the robot has for the person tends to be shallow (if any) and the social behavior is often pre-canned or reflexive"

(Breazeal, 2003, 169). In other words, these mechanisms act as if they are responding to the user, but this is an "act" or outward performance. A good example of this type of social robot are museum tour guides, interactive kiosks, and therapy robots, like Paro.

3. Socially Receptive—The robots in this category are also socially passive—insofar as they are not actively engaging people to satisfy their own social aims—but, unlike social interface devices, can benefit from the interactions they have with human users. This is accomplished by various learning capabilities, especially when it involves imitation. As Breazeal (2003, 169) explains: "Interactions with people affect the robot's internal structure at deeper levels, such as organizing the motor system to perform new gestures, or associating symbolic labels to incoming perceptions." Many of Breazeal's research robots, like Kismet and Leonardo, were designed to exhibit this capability.

4. Sociable—The sociable robot is described as being "socially intelligent in a human like way, and interacting with it is like interacting with another person" (Breazeal, 2002, 1). These devices just don't act or pretend to be social. They are, as Breazeal (2003, 169) explains, "socially participative 'creatures' with their own internal goals and motivations." Consequently, their social interactions not only benefit the user but also benefit the robot, e.g., promote its survival, improve its performance, and learn from the interaction. This is at the high end of the spectrum and would be populated by social robots that are (even at this time) more like the robots of science fiction than what many of us recognize as science fact.

As you move from the low to the high end of the scale, the robots become not only more capable but also more difficult to design and, as a consequence, more expensive to build. Fortunately, not every robotic device needs the full range of capabilities. In some situations (many situations, in fact) a reasonably believable appearance of social intelligence may be all that is necessary for the robot to establish and maintain the user's social expectations. This is relatively easy to accomplish in highly constrained situations and environments, as might be the case with a child's interactive toy. But as the variables in the environment or the tasks begin to increase in number and complexity, the social capabilities and functionality of the artifact will need to scale to meet user expectations.

4.2 EMBODIMENT AND MORPHOLOGY

Because the principal defining feature of the social robot is social interaction and communication, it is reasonable to ask: What makes a social robot different from a chatbot, an SDS application, or other socially interactive virtual entity, like an embodied conversational agent (ECA) or non-player character (NPC) in a virtual world or game? It's a reasonable question, because the line that separates "social robot" from these other socially interactive technologies is becoming increasingly difficult to define and defend. Is Siri, for instance, a social robot? Or is it just an SDS application residing in a number of different smart devices, like the iPhone? In most cases, the one criterion that is most often deployed to mark what differentiates chatbots and SDS from social robots is "embodiment."

4.2.1 EMBODIMENT

In the context of social robots, "embodiment" means more than just "having a (physical) body." Arguably an on-screen ECA or NPC possesses a kind of (virtual) body. Thus, it is possible to divide social robot embodiment into at least two varieties.

Virtual—Virtual social robots are like computer-controlled avatars. Replika, for instance, is a virtually embodied social robot that you can modify by selecting a wide range of options, including skin color, body type, and hairstyle. Consequently, in the same way that you can customize your avatar, you can design and redesign your Replika. It is this customizable virtual body that provides Replika with a much more robust set of communication capabilities and modalities that makes it more than just a chatbot or SDS application.

Physical—Other robots have physical bodies, like the Jibo robot that had been developed by Cynthia Breazeal. Jibo, unlike Replika, lives in the real world alongside us and not in a virtual world restricted to the screen. Thus, Jibo has a very real physical presence. At first look, the robot is about the same shape and size as an SDS smart speaker, those cylindrical tubes in which Alexa seems to be held captive. In fact, one of the factors that led to the commercial failure of Jibo was the fact that it hit the market around the same time that Amazon introduced the Alexa smart speaker. But unlike Jibo, Alexa was fraction of the cost.

What Jibo had going for it was its unique form of social presence. While the Alexa device just sat there, spitting out words, Jibo could move. When you talked, Jibo would pivot its head and make eye contact, meeting your gaze with what appeared to be a large cyclopic eye. When someone else in the room started talking, Jibo would change the direction of its gaze so as to signal to this other individual that Jibo not only recognized them but also was paying attention. When you said something funny, Jibo not only laughed but also displayed a smile on its faceplate. And when you told Jibo to dance, Jibo fired up the streaming media and moved to the beat. These non-verbals, especially movement and eye gaze, made Jibo a seemingly more competent conversational partner, even if Jibo was little more than a social interface device.

Hybrid—Finally, it should be noted that this virtual/physical distinction is not mutually exclusive. There are some social robots that combine the two forms of embodiment, like the Furhat robot (Figure 4.1). This robot has the physical form of a bust—the head and shoulders of a human figure—and a face that is rendered in video form by way of back projection. In this way, the Furhat

FIGURE 4.1 The Furhat robot.

Source: Photograph from https://furhatrobotics.com/get-furhat/basic-package/

robot leverages the advantages of both forms of embodiment. The robot has physical presence. It faces the user, and it has a face that can express a wide range of non-verbals. But unlike a physically embodied robot, the facial expressions of the Furhat device can be displayed and manipulated without intricate mechanical actuators or synthetic skin. Additionally, users can customize the look and features of their particular robot's face, including skin color, make-up, size of eyes, etc. This kind of customization would be both difficult and expensive for robots that are only physically embodied.

4.2.2 MORPHOLOGY

Morphology concerns the form or the shape of something. It is important in robotics, because the form or the shape that the robot takes helps establish and control for social expectations. If we encounter a robot that looks similar to a dog, we generally expect it to interact with us like a dog. Morphology, then, is one way that a social robot can communicate to us in its intended social role, function, and behavior. Social robots are typically categorized according to one of the three morphologies:

Zoomorphic—Many entertainment, personal, and toy robots emulate the look and feel of animals, including the hamster- or owl-looking Furby from Tiger Electronics, robot dogs like Sony's AIBO and Consequential Robotic's MiRo, Innvo Labs' animatronic dinosaur Pleo, and the seal-like therapy robot Paro. This morphology is expedient, because it calls upon and mobilizes a set of already established expectations and experiences that human beings have with other kinds of non-human creatures, like domestic animals and pets.

Because they emulate familiar non-human animals, these robots can be designed to be social and interactive without necessarily needing to produce human-level capabilities. This provides designers and the robot itself considerable latitude when it comes to engaging in effective social interactions. Paro, for instance, does not talk. But the device does produce seal-like noises as it is touched and manipulated. This limited range of communication abilities, which is, we should note, much easier to design for and incorporate in the device than a full NLP system, is entirely appropriate to the morphology of this artifact. It works, in other words, because human users would not expect a seal to be able to talk.

Caricatured—Cartoonists and animators have introduced and developed a wide range of animated objects that are believable social entities. Consequently, many experimental and commercially available social robots have been modeled on this morphology.

FIGURE 4.2 Kismet CC BY-SA 2.5.

Source: Photograph from https://commons.wikimedia.org/w/index.php?curid=374949

There is, for example, Breazeal's social robot prototype Kismet, which was a little more than a moveable robotic head possessing a gremlin-like appearance (Figure 4.2). Despite it rather rudimentary "intelligence"—or perhaps better stated, lack thereof—the programmed movement of Kismet's head and "facial features"—turning to look at you, raising its eyebrows, twisting its ears, etc.—were interpreted by human users as expressive and meaningful.

Anthropomorphic—At what many assume would be the "high end" of the social robot scale are humanoid robots—artifacts that are designed to look and function like human beings or quasi-human entities. This is seeded not only by science fiction, where robots have been "mechanical men" or automatons, but by the assumption that anything able to produce human social behaviors would need to be human-like in both structure and function.

Commercially, there are devices like NAO and Pepper from Softbank Robotics. NAO is a small (58 cm in height) bipedal humanoid robot that has been successfully used in education and healthcare. Pepper is a 120 cm robot on a wheeled platform. According to its marketing literature, "Pepper is the world's first social humanoid robot able to recognize faces and basic human emotions" (SoftBank Robotics, 2018).

There are also various human-looking humanoid robots, most of which are still in R&D platforms like Hiroshi Ishiguro's Geminoids and Sophia from Hanson Robotics. Geminoids are a teleoperated android twin of a real person. These robots, which are designed to emulate the appearance and behavior of their "source person," are covered with a pliable synthetic skin that is manipulated by subcutaneous actuators, providing the robot with the ability to reproduce human facial expressions. These robots are not autonomous; they are controlled, behind the scenes, by what are basically human puppeteers. Despite this, the social presence of these devices coupled with their verbal and non-verbal interpersonal communication abilities produce a rather uncanny experience that is virtually indistinguishable from that of another (real) human person.

Like the Geminoids, Sophia is also a humanoid robot covered in synthetic skin and able to interact with human users in both verbal and non-verbal modes. But unlike a teleoperated Geminoid,

Sophia is said to be controlled by a proprietary AI system that is designed to learn and evolve from interactions with human users. The robot was activated on 14 February 2016, and since that time has become something of a celebrity. She (and the robot has been deliberately gendered female) has appeared on a number of TV talk shows, addressed the United Nations, and is often invited to give keynote addresses at tech industry events and international meetings. In 2017, the Kingdom of Saudi Arabia granted Sophia honorary citizenship, making her "the first robot citizen."

4.3   OPPORTUNITIES AND CHALLENGES

As these artifacts come to occupy increasingly significant and influential positions in our world, positions where they are not just tools or instruments of human conduct and action but a kind of socially situated interactive entity in their own right, there are important opportunities and challenges that remain to be addressed and resolved. Many of these actually have little to do with the technical exigencies and design of systems. Instead, they involve the social circumstance, significance, and impact of these technologies.

4.3.1   *ANTHROPOMORPHISM AND THE UNCANNY VALLEY*

Let's begin with two issues that define what could be called "the problem space" of social robots. The first is anthropomorphism, which remains a hotly contested subject in the field. On the one hand, anthropomorphism is criticized for being a kind of deception that should be tightly controlled or even eliminated. What is needed, so the argument goes, is not only greater attention to transparency in design but also a concerted effort to avoid building things that encourage or otherwise support anthropomorphic projection in the first place.

But, and on the other hand, anthropomorphism has been proven to be extremely useful and expedient for creating socially engaging and interactive technology. So, instead of trying to eliminate it altogether, the goal should be to figure out ways to manage it for effective user experiences. In other words, since anthropomorphic projection is going to happen—whether we like it or not—it is better to learn how to work with it rather than struggling against it. The problem, then, is not that the potential for anthropomorphic projection exists; the problem is that we seem to be unable to decide whether such projections are detrimental, useful, or both, when it comes to robots that are designed for human communication and social interaction.

Whether this tendency to project human capabilities onto non-human things and objects is considered a good or bad thing, it is undoubtedly powerful. But this can go too far, producing another problem that is called the Uncanny Valley (Figure 4.3).

The "uncanny valley hypothesis" was initially proposed by the Japanese roboticist Masahiro Mori in 1970 in order to explain the "relation between the human likeness of an entity, and the perceiver's affinity for it" (Mori, 2012, 99). It states that as the appearance of an artifact (e.g., a robot, a prosthetic limb, or a puppet) comes closer to achieving human-like appearance, emotional response to

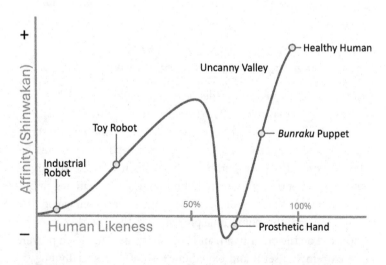

FIGURE 4.3 The Uncanny Valley as presented in Mori (2012).

the object is increasingly positive and empathetic. This correlation continues along a positive slope until the resemblance of the artifact becomes too close, and responses turn into revulsion, disgust, and rejection. But after this point, as the artifact's appearance comes so close to achieving human-like appearance as to be virtually indistinguishable from another human being, the response becomes positive again and eventually approaches human-to-human levels of affinity.

The uncanny valley hypothesis can, for example, explain why users find NAO to be an engaging and empathetic social partner while the RealDoll sex robot leaves many observers with a sense of creepiness and even disgust. Although Mori's proposal has never been definitively proven, his hypothesis has considerable traction, guiding not only the R&D efforts of roboticists, who try to design social artifacts that fall on either side of the valley, but also social scientists and communication researchers who employ the hypothesis as a way to explain and contextualize user responses to different kinds of socially interactive robots and artifacts.

4.3.2 REAL OR ILLUSION

One of the persistent and seemingly irresolvable issues with social robots is trying to decide whether these artifacts do in fact possess actual social intelligence, or whether this behavior is just a cleverly designed interface device that simulates various interpersonal effects that we—the human users—interpret as being social. And this difference matters, when it comes to social robots.

Sherry Turkle (2011), for one, worries that social robots deceive us, providing the illusion of interaction and connection without actually constituting a true social relationship. The problem, as Turkle describes it, is that the social bonds that develop between human users and robots will be asymmetrical or unidirectional with the human user investing heavily in the relationship and the robot not caring or worse not even caring that it is not caring.

This asymmetry has also got others concerned, like Matthias Scheutz, director of the human-robot interaction lab at Tufts University: "What is so dangerous about unidirectional emotional bonds is that they create psychological dependencies that could have serious consequences for human societies . . . Social robots that cause people to establish emotional bonds with them, and trust them deeply as a result, could be misused to manipulate people in ways that were not possible before. For example, a company might exploit the robot's unique relationship with its owner to make the robot convince the owner to purchase products the company wishes to promote" (Scheutz, 2012, 216–217). The problem, as Scheutz describes it, is that we—human users—might be (wrongly) attributing something to the robot that is not only one directional but also a potential for manipulation.

On the other side of the issue, however, there are various other voices that promote social robots not as a substitute for human sociability but as a means to understand, augment, and improve human social interactions and circumstances. The Paro robot has proven to be an incredibly useful tool in elder care, especially in situations involving individuals suffering from debilitating forms of dementia. In a number of clinical studies, the robot has been found to improve individual well-being by providing companionship and comfort in cases where other forms of interaction therapy are either difficult to provide or ineffectual. Social robots have also been shown to be expedient and effective tools for helping children with autism navigate the difficult terrain of human social interaction.

Beyond these therapeutic employments, however, social robots are both useful and entertaining. Many of us now have rudimentary social robots in our pockets and purses, with the smartphone being a kind of handheld companion robot that helps us connect to each other and our world. Even robots that are not explicitly designed for it can become social due to the role and function they play in human organizations. This is the case with many of the explosive ordinance disposal (EOD) robots used by soldiers on the battlefield. These miniature tank-like devices, which are clearly not designed for nor are outfitted with any of the programming and mechanisms for producing the effects of social interaction, occupy an important and valued position within the human combat unit. In fact, soldiers have formed surprisingly close personal bonds with their units' EOD robots, giving them names, awarding them battlefield promotions, risking their own lives to protect that of the robot, and even mourning their death. And at the other end of the spectrum, there are sex robots, which are being promoted not as substitutes for human partners but as a means to augment human intimacy and sexual relationships. In these cases, whether the robot is a genuine social entity or not seems less important than the net effects of its social presence and interactions—even if just simulated—on the human users who engage with it.

4.3.3 THING, PERSON, OR OTHERWISE

Social robots are a curious sort of thing. On the one hand, they are designed and manufactured technological artifacts. They are things. And like any of the other things that we encounter and use each and every day, they are objects with instrumental value. Yet on the other hand, these things are not quite like other things. They seem to have social presence, they are able to talk and interact with us, and many are designed to mimic or simulate the capabilities and behaviors that are commonly associated with human beings or animals.

So are social robots things, technological objects that we can use or even abuse as we decide and see fit? Or is it the case that these robots can or even should be something like a person—that is, another subject who would need to be recognized as a kind of socially significant other? These questions, which have been a staple in science fiction since the moment the robot stepped foot on the stage of history, are no longer a matter of fictional speculation. They are science fact and represent a very real legal and philosophical dilemma.

Resolving this seems pretty simple. All that would be needed is to assemble the facts and evidence, develop a convincing case, and then decide whether to categorize social robots as one or the other. This is not just good reasoning: it's the law. In fact, the binary distinction separating who is a person from what is a thing has been the ruling conceptual opposition in both moral philosophy and jurisprudence for close to 2,000 years. As Roberto Esposito (2015, 16), who arguably wrote the book on this subject explains: "From time immemorial our civilization has been based on the most clear-cut division between persons and things. Persons are defined primarily by the fact that they are not things, and things by the fact that they are not persons."

Consequently, all that is needed is to decide whether social robots should be classified as things or persons. Sounds easy enough, but it is much easier said than done. In fact, the social robot does not quite fit in or easily accommodate itself to either category. In a promotional video that was designed to raise capital investment through pre-orders, social robotics pioneer Cynthia Breazeal introduced her Jibo robot with the following explanation:

> This is your car. This is your house. This is your toothbrush. These are your things. But these [and the camera zooms into a family photograph] are the things that matter. And somewhere in between is this guy. Introducing Jibo, the world's first family robot.
>
> (Jibo, 2014)

Although this is just a marketing video, it does some impressive heavy lifting with regard to the perceived status of the social robot. In the video, Jibo is described as being not just another thing, like the automobile or toothbrush. But he/she/it (and the choice of pronoun is not unimportant in this context) is also not quite another member of the family pictured in the photograph. The robot inhabits a place in between these two mutually exclusive categories. It is neither/nor and both/and. This is, it should be noted, not unprecedented. We are already familiar with other entities that occupy a similar ambivalent social position, like the family dog. In fact, animals, as Kate Darling (2021) details in her book *The New Breed*, provide a good precedent for understanding the changing nature of things in the face of social robots.

Jibo, and other robots like it, are not science fiction. They are already or will soon be in our lives and in our homes. In the face of these socially situated and interactive technologies, we—individually and together—are going to have to decide whether they are mere things like our car, our house, and our toothbrush; someone who matters like another person or member of the family; or something altogether different that is situated in between the one and the other. In whatever way this comes to be decided, however, these things will undoubtedly challenge the way we typically distinguish between who is to be considered another social subject and what remains a mere thing or object.

The good news for students and professionals in the field of communication is that this effort is going to require not just innovation in the technology of AI and robotics but also extensive experience with and a deep understanding of human sociality. Consequently, there is a real need—an important and pressing need—for social scientists and humanists to join these conversations and to work with the engineers and designers to decide together not only what can be done with social robots but also what should be done to ensure that we foster the kind of world we want for ourselves and our robots.

5

LARGE LANGUAGE MODELS

Large language models (LLMs) are a recent innovation in NLP technology that employ transformer architectures that are pretrained on massive amounts of digital text scraped from the Internet. As a result, applications like OpenAI's GPT series as well as Google's LaMDA (Language Model for Dialogue Applications) and BERT (Bidirectional Encoder Representations from Transformers) can generate original text content that is, in many cases, indistinguishable from human written material. In effect, LLMs are NLP applications on steroids.

This chapter will (1) demystify the technology of LLMs by explaining the inner workings of these algorithms, (2) evaluate the costs and benefits of machine-generated content in different areas of human communication, and (3) explore the impact these technologies are likely to have on writing and its future. In effect, the chapter asks and seeks to respond to these questions: Does an LLM application like ChatGPT write? Do these algorithms know or understand what they are saying? And if so (or if not), how will this affect and/ or alter our understanding of human communication and writing?

5.1 DEMYSTIFYING LLMS

For those of us who are not data scientists or machine learning developers, the technology behind LLMs can seem a bit mysterious and unapproachable. So, let's begin by demystifying

DOI: 10.1201/9781003442240-5

the technology and seeing what actually goes on inside the "black box."

5.1.1 LANGUAGE MODEL

A language model is a probabilistic representation of a natural language. As we already saw with MT (Chapter 2), different sequences of characters that make up words and words that make up phrases are more likely to occur than other sequences, and these probabilities can be ranked and represented by numbers. A good illustration of how this works is to look at something with which we are all very familiar, the autocomplete function that is built into our mobile devices.

When you begin typing a word in your text messaging app, for instance, the device is able to predict or make a reasonable guess about the word you want even before you finish writing it. This is due to the fact that human languages can be statistically analyzed and processed. When you set out to type the word "type," for instance, you begin with "ty." The autocomplete algorithm makes a prediction about the next letter by consulting a list of probable sequences. Something like this:

tye	0.0000051%
type	0.0148257%
tycoon	0.0000375%
typhoon	0.0000396%
typography	0.0000397%

Here you can see that the next most often occurring letters in a sequence that begins with "ty" are "pe," thus autocompleting your text entry and providing the word "type." Of all the possible sequences of letters in English, "type" has the highest probably.

Language modeling involves predicting the next most probable element in a sequence, whether that sequence concerns letters that make up a word or words that make up a phrase. The language model is the statistical ranking of these various sequences, and that ranking is obtained from analyzing large amounts of human written material that is available in digital form on the Internet. The autocomplete algorithm, then, does not "understand" what it is you want to say. It simply takes the input, cycles through a set of available sequences, and identifies the one that is assigned the highest probability. This does not mean that the autocomplete is always correct in its prediction, and we have all experienced instances when the algorithm gets it wrong. But most of the time it is pretty accurate due to the fact that human languages are probabilistic.

Developing a language model requires that we assign a probability score (P) to different sequences of words in a particular language. Basically, something like this:

To be or not to be. That is the question. P = 0.003456%
Coffee sky would towards fun under.   P = 0.000006%

But if we try to do this for every possible sequence that could be made, we get a number that is astronomically large: 10^{50}, which as you may remember from your high school mathematics course is a 10 with 50 zeros after it. We can reduce this number by eliminating sequences that are grammatically incorrect or simply nonsense. Doing so, however, requires that we model not just possible word sequences but also grammar, style, and other elements that make language work. This requires that we develop a more complex model, and we can, once again, illustrate how this is done by using an example.

Consider the following word sequence derived from the book of *Genesis* in both the Christian and Jewish scriptures:

Now the earth was formless and empty, darkness was over the surface of the deep, and the Spirit of God was hovering over the waters.

Each word in this sequence depends on the one that comes directly before it. The word "was," for instance, depends on "earth" and

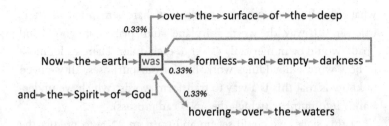

FIGURE 5.1 Language model with dependencies.

the word "formless" depends on the word "was." But there are also repetitions of the word "was" in the passage. So, we can economize things by merging the three instances of "was" and apply probabilities to these different dependencies or edges (Figure 5.1).

When we do this, we not only reduce the number of probable sequences that need to be modeled, but we can use these dependencies to generate other sequences of words that have a high probability of being valid sentences.

Now the earth was hovering over the waters.
And the Spirit of God was formless and empty.

5.1.2 TRANSFORMER ARCHITECTURE AND OPERATIONS

Modeling these dependencies is better than trying to model all possible word sequences but even then, the number is still too large for us to handle. We can resolve this problem by using an artificial neural network (ANN) to approximate these dependencies for us.

In order to do this, we first need to turn words into numbers that can be processed by an ANN. This could be done by numbering every word alphabetically so that the indefinite article "a" would be 0 and something like "zygote" would be 349,697. But then synonyms like "beautiful" and "pretty" or antonyms like "bad" and "good" would be very far apart from each other. A better way to do this is to use word embedding that assigns similar numbers—or what are called "vectors"—to words that share semantic character-istics. In this way, the words "airplane" and "plane" or "good" and "bad" would be numerically closer to each other. There's a lot more to how word embeddings work. But for our purposes, all we need to know is that this is a way to transform words (which we under-stand) into number (which the ANN can process).

At this stage, we could set up and train an ANN to predict the next word in a sequence by feeding it lots of word sequences—in the form of numbers that we have derived from the word embed-dings—and adjusting the weights on the connections between the individual neurons in the network. But it turns out that getting a single ANN to do this, even a really complex ANN with lots of hidden layers, is still too difficult a task. So we need to reduce the complexity of things.

To do this, we can capitalize on another feature of human lan-guage. Let's use another example, in this case a well-known rhyme that is missing the last word in the sequence.

Twinkle, twinkle, little star.
How I wonder what you ___.

Even if you had never heard this particular rhyme, there is a good chance that you could make a reasonable prediction about the miss-ing word. In fact, you could probably do it with only a few pieces of information:

_____, _____, _____ star.
____ _ _____ what you ___.

In predicting and completing word sequences, then, we do not need to pay attention to every single word and its dependencies. We can limit our attention to just a few crucial words. And we can do the same for our algorithm by adding an attention network to the word prediction ANN. This combination is called a "transformer," which is the "T" part of the acronym GPT.

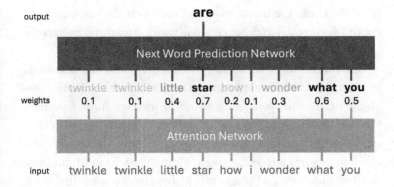

FIGURE 5.2 Transformer diagram.

Here's how it works. The attention network takes the input words and assigns each one an attention value or weight in the range of 0 to 1. These weights are determined by the relationship each word has to other words, producing something called a "context vector." And the attention network formulates a context vector for each word in the statement. It then multiplies these weights by the numeric value of the words themselves. This way, the attention words are given attention, i.e., their numeric value is increased, while the attention on other words is decreased (Figure 5.2).

Like all ANNs, the attention network needs to be trained. The training of the attention network could proceed by having human beings annotate rhymes and other word sequences, but this would be both tedious and expensive. A better way to proceed is to train both networks together, allowing the prediction network to tell the attention network what it needs in order to make better predictions.

If, for example, the prediction network spits out the word "potato" instead of "are," this error can be identified by comparing the output of the prediction network to the desired result and then readjusting the weights in the attention network, increasing the numeric value on the word "star" and decreasing the weights on other words that might have contributed to the erroneous output. This process is called "backpropagation" because the resulting error is fed back into the transformer and used to make adjustments to the weighted values in the attention network. And this is an iterative process that goes through hundreds of thousands of cycles.

One transformer may be adequate for predicting the next word in a simple rhyme, but it is not sufficient for tackling more complicated tasks, like generating an email message from a prompt. We can, therefore, expand its capabilities by stacking up layers of transformers, such that the output of one becomes the input for the other. In this arrangement, lower levels in the stack can handle basic word relationships and syntax and higher layers can be directed at more complex relationships, like semantics. It is this density that allows the stack of transformers to generate all kinds of different word sequences from a user prompt. This is the G part of the acronym GPT. So how many layers are we talking about? GPT-3 has 96 layers and its successor GPT-4 boasts 1.8 trillion parameters across 120 layers. This is what make these language models *large*.

Once these generative transformer systems are built, however, they need to be trained. This is the "P" part of the GPT acronym—pretrained. In order to do this, LLM developers need text—lots of text—meaning not only all of the Internet but also every publicly available book and document that exists in digital form. In effect, tech companies like OpenAI and Google have trained their LLM algorithms by scraping text data from every conceivable corner of the digital universe. This includes both public domain documents and material that is protected by copyright.

Processing this massive amount of data takes time and resources. It is estimated that training an LLM the size of GPT-3 on a single GPU would take 355 years. But transformers are designed to be operated in parallel, which means that the same task can be accomplished in about a month with several thousand GPUs. But doing so requires loads of digital equipment, data centers, electricity, and water for cooling the server clusters, which is why these models (so far at least) are only able to be developed and supported by corporations like OpenAI, Google, and Microsoft.

5.2 COST/BENEFIT ANALYSIS

Though many of the technological innovations behind LLM AI have been around for years, publicly available applications of these technologies are a rather recent development. And everything seems to begin on the 30th of November 2022, the day that OpenAI launched ChatGPT. After that date, ChatGPT and competing LLMs from Google, Anthropic, and others have been everywhere, and advocates and critics have lined up either to sing their praises— some even going so far as to claim that what we see in LLMs are "sparks of AGI" (Bubeck et al., 2023)—or issue dire warnings about social impact and costs.

5.2.1 LLM BENEFITS

LLMs are powerful applications capable of generating human-like textual content from a simple prompt. As such, they can perform a wide range of tasks, including but not limited to:

- **Text Generation**: LLMs can create coherent and contextually relevant text on a wide array of topics, ranging from creative writing (such as stories, poems, and song lyrics) to generating articles or essays on specific subjects.
- **Conversation**: These models can engage in dialogue, providing responses to questions, participating in discussions, and even simulating conversational partners in various scenarios.
- **Language Translation**: LLMs are capable of translating text from one language to another, facilitating communication across different linguistic backgrounds.
- **Information Summarization**: They can summarize lengthy documents, articles, or discussions, extracting key points and presenting them in a concise manner.
- **Question Answering**: LLMs can provide answers to questions posed by users, ranging from simple factual queries to more complex problem-solving tasks.

- **Text Completion and Suggestion:** They can complete partial sentences or suggest how a piece of text might continue based on the given context.
- **Sentiment Analysis:** LLMs can analyze text to determine the sentiment expressed, such as positive, negative, or neutral tones.
- **Grammar and Style Correction:** These models can suggest corrections for grammatical errors and offer stylistic improvements in writing.
- **Educational Assistance:** LLMs can be used for tutoring or providing explanations on a wide range of subjects, offering personalized learning support.
- **Content Curation and Recommendation:** They can assist in curating content tailored to individual preferences or generating personalized recommendations.

This list of capabilities is impressive. Maybe even more impressive is the fact that it was generated by ChatGPT from the prompt: "Briefly describe what LLMs can do." Even though ChatGPT does not know or understand the meaning of the sentences that it generates, the sequences of words that it arranges are meaningful and understandable by us and therefore appear to respond to the prompt.

5.2.2 LLM COSTS

Despite remarkable capabilities across a wide range of communication tasks, these technologies also have a number of limitations and challenges.

- **Bias**—LLMs can inherit and even amplify biases that are present in their training data. Since the source of the bias is in the data and the data is vast, both developers and users are typically not aware of the problem until the algorithm starts generating text and spitting out statements that are or at least could be interpreted as sexist, racist, ageist, ableist, etc. Fixing this problem is not easy, because the bias ultimately resides in the word dependencies that are contained in the training data. Consequently, solving this involves mobilizing a number of different strategies and approaches: data curation, model fine tuning, and output filtering.

- **Hallucinations**—In the context of LLM AI, "hallucination" refers to situations when an LLM produces text outputs that look legit—that is, the text is coherent, well-composed, and grammatically correct—but are factually wrong, fabricated, or nonsensical. LLMs have generated academic papers that make reference to sources that do not exist. They have written recipes that include ingredients that are not fit for human consumption. And they have produced financial reports, where most of the data has been fabricated. This problem is not a matter of the LLM making a mistake or intentionally lying. They are as incapable of fabricating falsehoods as they are of telling the truth. Despite this fact, LLM hallucinations can be a problem for individuals and organizations that rely on the algorithm to produce content. Like bias, this problem only becomes evident in the output, and then only by scrutinizing the results and performing a thorough fact check. And fixing the problem is just as difficult, requiring a similar set of strategies.

- **Intellectual Property**—Training LLMs requires massive amounts of textual data. Basically every piece of writing that resides on the Internet and all books and documents that are available in digital form. But not all text is created equal. Some text, like government documents and literary classics from the past, are public domain, meaning that this textual data can be copied and reused without infringing on anyone's intellectual property. Other texts are protected by copyright and therefore can only be reused by others if one obtains permission or negotiates a licensing agreement. And it turns out that LLMs, like OpenAI's GPT series, may have been trained on digital text without paying attention to or differentiating the one category of text from the other.

This has recently blown up with authors, journalists, screen-writers, and publishers complaining that OpenAI has been using their content without consent, compensation, or credit (what is now being called the three Cs). This is the point of contention in a lawsuit brought by The New York Times against OpenAI and Microsoft. In their filing in the US District Court of Southern New York (Case 1:23-cv-11195), the Times alleges that OpenAI and Microsoft used the news organization's copyrighted content to train their LLMs and as such not only violated copyright but also now facilitate the production of content that unfairly competes with the news organization (The New York Times Company v. Microsoft Corporation, 2024). OpenAI has defended its actions and sought protection under the fair use exception that is contained in US copyright law. It has further argued that compensating publishers, like The New York Times, for its use of text content would render the training of LLMs prohibitively expensive and hinder technological progress.

- **Environmental Impact**—Even though you access ChatGPT on your mobile device, the algorithm does not reside in your phone. It is a cloud-distributed application that is accessed by your device over a network connection to the Internet. The word "cloud" actually does a lot of heavy lifting here. It gives the impression of something residing in the heavens. But this is a myth—a myth that conceals the true cost and consequences of these innovations. Cloud-distributed services are not disembodied technological spirits residing in the air. They have a very real, physical presence—specifically server clusters that consume large amounts of electrical power and need to be cooled down with water.

  According to Sajjad Moazeni, a researcher at Washington University, ChatGPT responds to hundreds of millions of queries per day. At this rate, he estimates that the servers supporting the algorithm consume approximately 1 GWh per day, which is equivalent to the daily energy consumption for about 33,000 US households (McQuate, 2023). Rapid growth in this sector has led other researchers to predict that by 2027, AI servers could use between 85 and 134 terawatt hours (Twh) annually, which is similar to what Argentina, the Netherlands, and Sweden each use in a year (de Vries, 2023). These are, it should be pointed out, all estimates made by researchers. The exact figures are actually difficult to obtain, because there are—in the United States, at least—no federally stipulated rules or guidelines for reporting this information. But it is telling that OpenAI CEO, Sam Altman, has said that the continued development of LLM AI will not be possible without a new breakthrough in energy generation (Tangermann, 2024).

Water is also an issue. ChatGPT may have been developed in San Francisco, but it resides in Des Moines, where the server cluster supporting the LLM quenches its thirst on the Midwest's rather ample supply of clean, fresh water. In response to a lawsuit filed by local residents, it was revealed that the training of this powerful generative AI system consumed 6% of the district's water. This number may not seem like a lot, but it tells us two things: First, AI is thirsty and its need for water is only going to increase. How much and what this means is the second item, as there are again no federal regulatory standards for reporting and evaluating the environmental impact of these technologies.

• **Technological Unemployment**—LLM AI certainly poses a threat of technological unemployment, especially in industries and for occupations that deal with communication. When an algorithm like ChatGPT can produce legible content for publication or chat with customers in real time, the need for human writers—journalists, copywriters, authors, and scriptwriters—and for corporate communication professionals is going to take a hit. During the last disruption to the industry—the Internet—the usual advice given to displaced workers was to learn how to code, and many answered the call by learning the core technologies of HTML, CSS, and JavaScript. But that is no longer a solution as ChatGPT can write executable code from either a prompted description or even a sketch of the user interface for a web app.

Responses to this impending crisis have taken a number of different forms. One approach is to push back. This is precisely what happened with the Hollywood writers' strikes of 2023. In their contract negotiations with the studio, the Writers Guild of America demanded protections against AI-generated content, especially training LLMs on the writers' own screenplays and then having to compete against the algorithm for future work. The writers guild was successful in obtaining these guarantees, but this was only possible because they were represented by a powerful union that was able to secure these protections through collective bargaining. Other workers in other fields—like legal assistants, PR copywriters, and journalists—may not have the same opportunity. Unlike unionized workers, they may find themselves facing these challenges alone and feeling rather powerless to do anything about it.

Another approach is reskilling. LLMs might be taking over many of the writing and content generation tasks once performed by human workers, but these technologies have also created some new opportunities, like prompt engineer. Thus, so the argument goes, all that displaced human workers need to do is develop a new (albeit related) skill set and re-band themselves as prompt engineers. There are two issues here. First, we have numbers problem. Whereas advertising or PR agencies might have employed 15–20 copywriters, they probably will be able to get by with only 1 or 2 prompt engineers. Since automation aims to economize labor—i.e., reduce the labor force—this is not going to be a 1:1 substitution. Consequently, there will be less opportunities and therefore greater competition for the smaller number of available openings.

Second, it is, at this time at least, unclear as to what skills a prompt engineer needs to be successful. This is understandable, mainly because the position did not exist until very recently, and we are, in effect, making things up as we go along. This means that displaced human workers not only need to reskill but also may need to do so without knowing for sure what exact skills are going to matter or make a difference. It also means that colleges, universities, and tech schools need to begin reworking the curriculum to address and cultivate these capabilities.

5.3 DOES WRITING HAVE A FUTURE?

One of the main complaints or criticisms directed against LLMs, like OpenAI's ChatGPT and Google Gemini, is that these technologies generate seemingly intelligible statements, but they do not and cannot understand what they say. Versions of this have proliferated in both the academic and popular media. If this way of thinking sounds familiar, it should. It's just good old fashioned logocentric thinking. *Logocentrism* is one of those -isms that proliferate in heady philosophical discussions about language. But what it identifies is rather intuitive: Writing is the product of an author—someone who it is assumed has something meaningful to say by way of the written artifact. The fundamental challenge with LLMs is that these algorithms disturb this usual way of thinking. And this has at least three important consequences.

5.3.1 DEATH OF THE AUTHOR

Despite appearances, the concept "author" is not some naturally occurring phenomenon or universal truth. It is a socially constructed subject position. In fact, as literary scholars have documented, written texts only came to have authors—in the way we today understand that word—during the modern era, and they did so in response to problems having to do with the identification and assignment of responsibility in the wake of a prior technological disruption—the printing press.

But if the author—as the principal figure of modern literary authority—comes into existence at a particular time and place, there is also a point at which it may cease to fulfill this role. It is this passing away of the figure of the author that is announced and marked by Roland Barthes's seemingly apocalyptic essay, "Death of the Author." Although Barthes could not have addressed LLMs, his work on authorship expertly anticipates our current situation. It is with LLM applications like ChatGPT that we now confront texts that have no identifiable author. Such writings are literally *unauthorized*. But instead of this being a criticism concerning what these AI-generated texts lack, it shows us the extent to which the authority for writing—any writing whether human or machine—has always and already been a socially constructed artifice.

5.3.2 THE MEANS OF MEANING

Once writing is cut loose from the controlling interests and intentions of an author, the question concerning significance gets turned around. Specifically, the meaning of a text is not something that can be guaranteed in advance by the authentic subjectivity of the one who is assumed to be speaking through the medium of the writing. Meaning emerges in and from the process of reading.

This shifts the location of meaning-making from the original intentions of the author/writer to the interpretive activity of the reader who finds meaning in or generates it from the materiality of the text. As Barthes (1978, 148) explains:

> Text is made of multiple writings, drawn from many cultures and entering into mutual relations of dialogue, parody, contestation, but there is one place where this multiplicity is focused and that place is the reader . . . A text's unity lies not in its origin but in its destination.

After the "death of the author," what a text comes to mean is not guaranteed by the authentic subjectivity of an author who expresses themselves in and by writing. It is something that is situated on the side of reception in the readers and the performance of reading. While the significance that emerges in this process is customarily attributed to the original intentions of an author, that attribution is fabricated out of an act of reading. Thus, meaning is actually (and has always been) an effect that has been retroactively projected to become its own presumed cause.

5.3.3 WORDS AND THINGS

Finally, the issue is not (at least not exclusively) where meaning is located and produced. What is at issue is the concept of meaning itself. Since at least Aristotle, language has been understood to consist of signs that refer and defer to things. Following this classical semiology (aka "theory of meaning"), it has been argued that LLMs do not truly comprehend the meaning behind the words, because they have no access to real-world referents. In other words, they manipulate signs without knowing that to which these tokens refer (or do not refer, which amounts to the same thing).

This seemingly common-sense view, however, is not necessarily the natural order of thing. And it has been directly challenged by more recent innovations in structural linguistics, which see language and meaning-making as a matter of difference situated within language itself. The dictionary provides what is perhaps one of the best, if not the best, illustrations of this basic semiotic principle. In a dictionary, words come to have meaning by way of their relationship to other words. In pursuing definitions of words in the dictionary, one remains within the system of linguistic signifiers and never gets outside language to the referent or what semioticians call the "transcendental signified."

What this means is that a text—whether it is written by a human being or artificially generated by an LLM (with the nudge of a human supplied prompt)—comes to have meaning not by referring and deferring to some transcendental signified. It comes to enact and perform meaning by way of interrelationships to other texts and contexts in which it is already situated and from which it draws its discursive resources. Consequently, what has been offered as a criticism of LLM technology—namely, that these algorithms only circulate different signs without access to the signified—might not be the indictment critics think it is. As viewed from the perspective of recent innovations in linguistics, this is an accurate diagnosis of how language actually functions.

6

COMPUTATIONAL CREATIVITY
AND GENERATIVE AI

Even if AI automates a wide range of the routine and repetitive tasks in many areas of human communication—like translating between languages, summarizing human written documents, and participating in basic interpersonal interactions—it seems a safe bet to assert that they will never be able to do something inventive, innovative, and inspirational. They will, in other words, never be able to do what we do, i.e., be genuinely creative and to produce something completely new and original. Right? Maybe not.

This chapter (1) investigates whether, and to what extent, AI applications and devices can be considered "creative" in a wide range of activities; (2) details and investigates the technological features and functions of specific computational creativity systems, especially recent innovations in diffusion models and transformer architectures, like Midjourney, Dall-E, Stable Diffusion, and Sora; and (3) demonstrates how and why these innovations necessitate critical reflection on the concept and meaning of human creativity. The guiding questions of this chapter are: Can AI be creative? And, if so, what does that mean for us—specifically those of us who work or seek to work in one of the creative industries, like music, filmmaking, storytelling, visual art and design, etc.?

DOI: 10.1201/9781003442240-6

6.1 AUTOMATED CREATIVITY

Creativity does not happen in a vacuum. A creative artist is always calling on, borrowing from, and recombining elements drawn from works produced by their predecessors. Perhaps the most direct articulation of this can be found in a formula developed by Kirby Fergusson in his web documentary *Everything Is a Remix*. According to Ferguson (2014), all acts of creativity in all forms of art can be described by three, recursive operations: copy, transform, and combine. Like all formulas or recipes, this is actually an algorithm for creating "new" works of art, and, like any algorithm, it can be and has been made computable.

6.1.1 MUSIC

Though there have been numerous experiments with algorithmic composition and performance—extending from the musical dice game or *Musikalisches Würfelspiel* of 18th century Europe to computer implemented composition techniques in the 20th century—one of the most celebrated achievements in the field has been David Cope's Experiments in Musical Intelligence, EMI or "Emmy." Emmy was a PC-based algorithmic composer that was capable of analyzing existing musical compositions, rearranging their basic components, and then generating new, original scores that sound like and in some cases are indistinguishable from the master works of Mozart, Bach, and Chopin.

The inner workings of Emmy are quite simple. As Cope (2017) described it on his website, the algorithm works using three basic principles:

1. *Deconstruction* (analyze and separate into parts)
2. *Signatures* (commonality—retain that which signifies style)
3. *Compatibility* (recombinancy—recombine into new works)

Like all algorithmic applications, Emmy needs to be supplied with computable musical data. For this purpose, Cope designed a special data structure for music, where each note in a given musical work would be represented by a distinct set of five numbers that could then be stored in a database and processed by the Emmy algorithm. In his book, *Virtual Music*, Cope (2001, 142) provides the following example:

(0 60 1000 1 64)

This is the numeric representation of one musical event—a note. Though Cope does not use the term in his own writings on the subject, it is a musical note embedding. The first number (0) represents the event's "on-time" or the amount of time that has elapsed from the beginning of the work to the time that the note is initiated. The second number (60) represents pitch. The third number (1000) indicates duration—how long a note is held. The fourth (1) represents the number of the MIDI channel that is assigned to that note for the purposes of its performance. And the fifth and final number (64) represents dynamics with 0 indicating silence and 127 being fortissimo. Using this numeric representation, one can transpose a musical composition into a sequence of numbers, or what Cope calls an "event list," that can then be accessed and processed by the Emmy algorithm.

Once different musical compositions have been translated into event lists and stored in the database, the Emmy algorithm proceeds through four sequentially ordered processing steps.

1. Pattern Matching—Once different musical works have been translated into a common method of numeric representation, you can use simple pattern matching techniques to identify commonalities (similar kinds of numbers) between different works, which is an indicator of the "style" of a particular composer (e.g., Bach) or genre of music (e.g., a Baroque chorale).
2. Segmentation—In order to recombine different musical phrases, you need to break the work apart into segments. But simply extracting and then reordering different musical segments risks producing musical gibberish. For this reason,

Emmy applies an additional analytical step, appending a SPEAC score—Statement, Preparation, Extension, Antecedent, and Consequent—to each one of the extracted segments. The SPEAC score ensures that the recombined segments are ordered in such a way that they sound right, i.e., the ending of one segment leads into the next segment in a way that makes sense musically.

3. Recombination—Recombinancy is a rule-based process for organizing existing data into new sequences. These rules—basic guidelines or principles governing musical qualities like pitch, melody, harmony, etc.—can be preprogrammed, but this produces results that usually sound mechanical. For this reason, Emmy utilizes recombination rules that are not imposed by the programmer but discovered in the genre and style of the source material. Emmy acquires its rules by utilizing Augmented Transition Networks (ATNs), which were initially developed in NLP for parsing (taking apart and analyzing) natural language sentences. Emmy uses ATN to analyze the logical order of segments in the music that is stored in the database in order to identify recombination rules that are consistent with the musical form, style, or genre it is emulating.

4. Output—The output of the Emmy software is a new musical composition that is stylistically faithful to but different from compositions in the database. This output can be manifested in the form of a musical score that can be played by human musicians or a MIDI file that can be processed by a computer-controlled synthesizer.

Cope has tested and proven Emmy's capabilities by deploying a remixed version of Alan Turing's game of imitation. This game, as Cope describes it, asks groups of people to listen to different musical compositions. Some of the compositions are works composed by human beings, e.g., chorales by J. S. Bach or mazurkas by Frédéric Chopin, and others are similar kinds of works generated by Emmy. The objective of the game is to see what percentage of listeners is able to distinguish the human-generated compositions from that created by the algorithm. And as Cope has discovered, listeners, even expert musicologists, have considerable difficulty with making the correct identification.

6.1.2 VISUAL ART

Cope's method for computational creativity is not limited to music. It can also be employed for and applied to any creative practice where new works are the product of reorganizing or recombining a set of finite elements, e.g., the 26 letters in the alphabet, the 12 tones in the musical scale, and the 16 million colors discernable by the human eye. Consequently, it should be no surprise that this approach to computational creativity has been implemented with other art works, like visual art.

A good example is The Painting Fool, which was developed by Simon Colton. To date the algorithm has produced hundreds of "original" artworks that have been exhibited in both online and real-world art galleries. Although the program and its mode of operations have been continually modified and upgraded over time, it also is built on and employs a form of decomposition and recombination, extracting images from the Internet, decomposing those images into useful visual segments by applying standard image manipulation tools, and then recombining these various elements on a two-dimensional grid.

Other approaches to creative content generation—especially but not necessarily limited to visual compositions—have exploited the artistic opportunities that are available with deep neural networks and connectionist architectures. The Paris-based art-collective Obvious (2018), for instance, has employed generative adversarial networks (GANs) in order to produce portraits of a fictional family (the Belamys) in the style of the European masters.

GANs are a form of unsupervised machine learning that employ two interconnected neural networks. One network, called the "generator," produces various candidates that seek to emulate a particular data distribution, like an image. In the case of Obvious, these data consisted of 15,000 portraits painted between the 14th and 20th centuries. The other network, called the "discriminator," evaluates the different candidates that have been generated in order to differentiate between images from the original data set and the various imitations produced by the generator. In the process, backpropagation is applied with both networks so that the generator produces increasingly better images, while the discriminator gets better at identifying the forgeries. In October of 2018, one of the works produced by this process, "Portrait of Edmond de Belamy," was auctioned by Christies and sold for just under half a million US dollars.

The most recent contenders in this domain are the text-to-image generators, like Dall-E, Midjourney, and Stable Diffusion. These applications—which are kind of like LLMs for images—are built on diffusion models. Diffusion models are a form of generative AI, meaning that they can be used to produce data similar to that on which they were trained. In this case, training consists of progressively destroying the training data. That is, we take an image and gradually degrade it by adding random noise, or what is commonly call "static," until we get something that results in pure Gaussian noise. We then reverse the process. That is, we begin with the noisy result and try to recreate the original from the static. In doing so, we will inevitably produce a variety of different images that are more or less like the original, and we can, by adjusting the weighted connections in the network, gradually have the model learn how to remove the noise and recover the original.

Once trained, the diffusion model can then be prompted to generate different kinds of images. If, for instance, we prompt Dall-E with "black and white photograph of a dog," the algorithm will generate an image of a dog. This is accomplished by combining the diffusion model with some text-to-image guidance. And there are different methods for doing this. Instead of trying to cover all of them, let's look at how this is implemented with OpenAI's Dall-E 2.

In an abstract sense (or what computer scientists routinely call the "highest level" description), Dall-E 2 consists of two basic

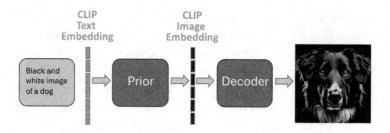

FIGURE 6.1 Block diagram of Dall-E 2.

operations. The first—called the "prior"—maps text embeddings (i.e., numeric representations of the prompt) onto image embeddings (i.e., numeric representations of an image) and the other—called the "decoder"—turns this image embedding into an actual image (Figure 6.1).

The text and image embeddings are generated by another model developed by OpenAI called CLIP (Contrastive Language–Image Pre-training). CLIP is a neural network model that can output the best (or most relevant) caption from a particular image. Show CLIP a black and white photo of a dog, and the algorithm will spit out something like "B&W image of a dog." In order to accomplish this, CLIP utilizes two encoders. One encoder turns images into image embeddings; the other one turns text into text embeddings.

What CLIP is designed to do is find the point of contact where the value of the text embedding is as close as possible to that of the image embedding. In order to accomplish this, CLIP needs to be trained on available image/caption pair. And like all machine learning systems, it needs a lot of these, basically hundreds of thousands of images that have been tagged with textual descriptions, like "image of a dog." And where does OpenAI obtain all these image/caption pairs? From the Internet, of course, and social media in particular. This means that all the effort you put into posting and captioning images on platforms like Instagram and Facebook is information and labor that is being used to train these models. We are working for the AI.

So now, if we put this all together, we can see how Dall-E 2 works. When you prompt the algorithm, the "prior" takes this prompt as input, turns it into a text embedding by using the CLIP text encoder, and maps it onto the closest associated image embedding as determined by the CLIP image encoder. The "decoder"—which is a diffusion model—takes the resultant image embedding as input and feeds this into the diffusion model to obtain an image. And because this is a diffusion model, we are not only able to reproduce images that look substantially similar to the training data but can also generate new images: e.g., different variations, combinations, and modifications.

6.2   OPPORTUNITIES AND CHALLENGES

Algorithms that produce music, visual images, and even video— whether they do so by using the GOFAI methods employed by David Cope and Simon Colton or mobilize the power of ANNs and recently developed generative models, like OpenAI's Dall-E and Sora or the audio diffusion applications of Suno and Udio—exhibit many of the same opportunities and challenges we already encountered in our examination of LLMs. This is because the general effect of text-to-music or text-to-image generation is very similar to that of text generation: It produces new and seemingly original content from a user supplied prompt. But is the output of these systems really new and original? Is this art? And if not, then what is it? These questions inevitably lead to some pretty deep philosophical issues regarding art and artistry.

6.2.1   ARTWORKS AND THE WORK OF THE ARTIST

One way we typically make sense of art and creativity is by appreciating the effort and talent of the artist who created the artwork— with an emphasis on the word "work" as making something like this typically requires both skill and labor. Generative AI messes with this idea. Users of these systems, even those lacking artistic skill, training, or talent, can now create stunning images and

FIGURE 6.2 Jason Allen's "Théâtre D'opéra Spatial" (2022).

audio/video contents quickly and easily. And that could be a problem. Consider Jason Allen's "Théâtre D'opéra Spatial," an award-winning artwork he developed by prompting Midjourney (Figure 6.2).

After his win, Allen posted a photo of the blue-ribbon prize and the award-winning artwork to Discord. News of this eventually made its way to Twitter (aka X), where it ignited a furor of criticism. Kevin Roose, a reporter for *The New York Times*, documented the fallout in an article titled "An A.I.-Generated Picture Won an Art Prize. Artists Aren't Happy" (2022). In the article, Roose quotes two posts that are indicative of the disapproval:

"We're watching the death of artistry unfold right before our eyes."

"This is so gross. I can see how A.I. art can be beneficial, but claiming you're an artist by generating one? Absolutely not."

Here we see a set of opportunities and challenges that are similar to what we discovered with LLMs. On the one hand, these technologies not only provide us with a powerful tool for creating artistic content, they also lower the bar for inclusion. They permit individuals who may have been excluded or marginalized from participation in various creative endeavors to make original content that they would not have otherwise been able to accomplish on their own. It has even been suggested that these technologies have the effect of democratizing content generation in art and design.

On the other hand, users of these technologies do not really need to know much as all that is necessary for success is that they prompt the algorithm. Consequently, users of Midjourney or Dall-E might create something that looks like art, but they certainly are not artists nor are they going to become artists as they are not developing their own skills, talents, and knowledge. Instead of putting in the work to make art, they are, it seems, taking the easy way out.

If this sounds familiar, it should. This is not only the terms of the debate that Plato (1982) recounts in the *Phaedrus* concerning the new technology of writing, it also characterizes what is said about other technological innovations that affect human creativity, like hip hop and other forms of remix. Hip hop radically reinvented how music is made. Unable to afford or otherwise acquire expensive musical instruments, the early innovators repurposed discarded consumer electronics and turned them into a new kind of musical instrument—one that could sample, loop, and recombine the best segments or hooks from prerecorded music. But the sampling and recombining of other artists' recordings was severely criticized as derivative, talentless, and lazy. The DJ was not considered to be a musician but was, in the words of punk and indie rock icon Henry Rollins (2007), little more than a "record player player." But just a few decades after DJ Kool Herc got things started, the techniques and technologies developed in hip hop and other remix practices have changed the artform and our understanding of how music is made.

6.2.2 ORIGINAL OR COPY

The accusation of "record player player" gets at another important aspect of art and artistry, and that is the difference between an original work and derivative copies. This applies not only to those things that rise to the level of a "work of art" but also to average everyday content, like student essays and projects. The standard plagiarism statement issued by universities encourage students to produce original work and not copy or pass off as their own content that which has been produced by others. And existing copyright statutes draw a line between an original creative work, which is protected by law, and copies of it, which are not only derivative but infringe on the rights and protections granted to the original.

This axiology or theory of value has deep roots going as far back as—and you can guess where this is going—Plato. In his writings, especially the *Republic* (Plato, 1987) and the *Phaedrus* (Plato, 1982), Plato distinguished between the singular original and its various copies. The former is the genuine and authentic article, whereas the latter is simply a cheap knock-off. But even if you have never read Plato, you already know this as it has framed the way we usually make sense of things. There's a difference between DaVinci's painting of the Mona Lisa that resided in the Louvre museum in Paris and the picture post-card reproductions of it that are sold in the gift shop. The former is a priceless work of art, whereas the latter costs a few Euros.

And the main issue here is similar to something we had confronted with remix at the turn of the century. In sampling and recombining existing content—like what DJ Danger Mouse famously did with his recombination of the Beatles and Jay Z—do we get something new and original? Or is it just a copy? Likewise, when David Cope prompts Emmy to fabricate a chorale in the style of J. S. Bach, is this a new work of classical music, or is it just a cheap imitation of the original? When I prompt Dall-E to generate an image of a robot in the style of DaVinci's Mona Lisa, have I created a new and original image, or is it a copy of copy, given that Dall-E's training data are not THE original artworks but digital copies of those works? (Figure 6.3).

The problem is that the jury is still out on all these questions. For some, what these machines produce are cheap imitations that infringe on the intellectual property rights of others, specifically actual human artists whose work may have been included in the training data without meeting the three C's of consent, credit, and compensation. For others, AI-generated content are truly

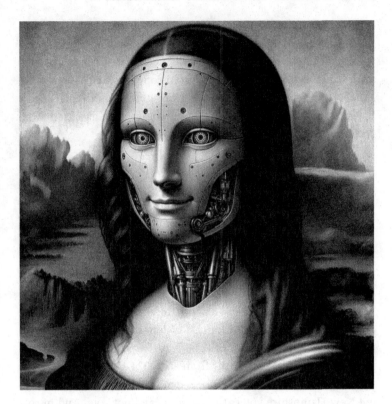

FIGURE 6.3 Dall-E-generated image from the prompt "Black and white portrait of a robot inspired by the style of DaVinci's Mona Lisa."

transformative works, which, like other creative practices, inevitably draw on what came before not in an effort to copy but to build on it and to invent something that is unique and original in its own right.

6.2.3 DEEPFAKES

In blurring the boundary that separates the original from its copies, generative AI also produces what French theorist Jean Baudrillard called "simulations." As Baudrillard explains, simulations are not copies or representations of originals, they deconstruct the very difference that had distinguished original from copy. Simulation, as Baudrillard (1994, 2) explains, is "the generation by models of a real without origin or reality," where the "sovereign difference" that had at one time distinguished original from copy has itself disappeared. Another (more negatively charged) word for this is "deepfake."

According to Wikipedia (2024)—a source that has itself been criticized as a platform for simulations—

> deepfakes (a portmanteau of the words "deep learning" and "fake") are synthetic media that have been digitally manipulated to replace one person's likeness convincingly with that of another. It can also refer to computer-generated images of human subjects that do not exist in real life.

Digitally manipulated images, video, and audio are not new. But deepfakes go further and examples are all too readily available. There is the famous video from 2016 that substituted the face and voice of Steve Buscemi for that of Jennifer Lawrence. There is that 2023 viral photograph of Pope Francis sporting a white puffy jacket. There is that robo-call from the 2024 US presidential primary race, in which President Joe Biden's voice was manipulated to tell New Hampshire voters to stay home and not vote. And in that same year, there were the deepfake pornographic videos of Taylor Swift that caught the attention not only of her fans but government regulators.

With generative AI, the creation of deepfakes is now easier than ever and virtually anyone can do it. In some instances, these synthetic images and sounds are entertaining and even funny. In other cases—like the Joe Biden robo-call—they can be dangerous and even threaten the integrity of the democratic process. But the real problem is not that deepfakes can momentarily fake us out; the problem is that the existence and proliferation of deepfakes desta- bilize the assumed relationship between media representations and reality. And this is especially true for those modes of media repre- sentation that are considered to be a faithful index of reality, i.e., photography, video, and sound recording. At this point in time, it is becoming increasingly difficult to decide if what is seen or heard is actually real or AI generated.

In responding to this crisis, the history of media technology can actually help us. Today we readily assume (almost without question) that a photograph is a faithful representation of reality. We take photos and make videos at concerts to show our friends (and even show off) that we were really there. We make selfies with celebrities to document the fact that we actually met them. And we use videos of protesters and police brutality in court cases as evidence of what really happened. But this has not always been the case. In fact, it is an idea that had to be developed and codified over time as people became more aware of and familiar with these technologies.

Today we take it for granted that a picture is an index or faithful representation of something that is really real. And we rarely question it. Deepfakes flip the script on us, challenging this very assumption and disorienting those of us who have come to put our faith in "seeing is believing." At this point in time, the rules of the game—at least as far as we thought we understood them—no longer apply. We now live in that hyperreality of simulation that Baudrillard had predicted back in the 1980s.

6.2.4 RESPONSIBILITY

With AI-generated content—whether it is an award-winning image or an audio deepfake—we often ask and inevitably want to know who (or even what) is to be credited or blamed. In other words, who's responsible? Who for, example, is the artist that can be credited with and compensated for the painting of Edmond de Belamy that had been auctioned by Christies? Is it the Obvious Collective? Is it the human individuals who make up this group? Is it the algorithm? Or is it, perhaps, a combination of these in a kind of hybrid of human and machine? The problem is that these questions not only lack an easy answer but seem to be getting more complicated and difficult to resolve.

Artists like Mark Amerika and Holly Herndon now talk about the AI as co-author and collaborator, while academic journals like *Springer Nature* now reserve the title "author" for human beings and deny attribution of authorship to the AI. When Jason Allen sought to register his AI-generated artwork for copyright protection, the US Copyright Office (USCO) ruled that the work "lacks human authorship" and therefore falls outside the purview of copyright law, which "excludes works produced by non-humans." Though this ruling seems to be a win for team human, there's more to it. In making this ruling, the USCO not only denied authorship to the AI but also denied the right of authorship to Allen, who prompted the Midjourney application. Steven Thaler, who has also sought both copyright and patent protections for AI-generated content, has had similar experiences. The result is that we now have what Thaler has called "orphaned art" that will lack any suitable IP (intellectual property) protections or guarantees for digital artists (Schrader, 2023). In effect, we now have artworks without there being anyone or anything who is responsible for it.

6.3   THE DIFFERENCE THAT MAKES A DIFFERENCE

In evaluating and trying to resolve these debates, we can clearly learn something from previous artistic disruptions, like dada, hip hop, and remix. But we should not be too quick to miss or dismiss what makes generative AI different. First, the DJ or remix artist was a kind of revolutionary figure pushing back against the culture industry with their DIY initiative and inventiveness. Generative AI systems, like OpenAI's Dall-E, is a corporate product. It belongs and is entirely beholden to highly profitable multinational corporations. Thus, the romantic image of the crate-diving DJ recovering deep cuts in prerecorded content from the past has now been replaced by the indiscriminate scaping of Internet content by big tech companies, who stand to make a lot of money off the effort. The practices may be similar, but the power dynamics are different.

Additionally, and this is the second point, there is a difference in the raw material. In remix the fundamental unit of analysis is the sample. "Sampling as an act," as remix theorist Eduardo Navas (2012, 11–12) explains,

> is basically what takes place in any form of mechanical recording—whether one copies by taking a photograph, or cuts, by taking a part of an object or subject, such as cutting part of a leaf to study under a microscope.

Earlier forms of computational creativity—in NLP applications like ELIZA and GOFAI machine-generated visual art like Simon Colton's The Painting Fool—worked with a similar formulation. Generative AI and diffusion models, however, are different. Unlike remix—whether human directed or computationally actualized—generative AI applications work with statistical data derived from massive amounts of available examples. This data is not a sample in the technical sense of the word; it is a series of numbers—a statistical vector or embedding—representing individual differences (e.g., in pixel saturation and brightness) that describe the basic elements of the original content.

Thus, generative AI introduces an additional level of abstraction away from the content that comes to be appropriated and used. In other words, we do not make a decisive cut out of the original in the way that sampling does. Instead, we use the data that describe the original to train a generative model that then is set up to produce similar kinds of data formations based on a prompt. Holly Herndon and Mat Dryhurst have named this "spawning" in an effort to distinguish what happens in generative AI from what occurs with sampling in both analog and digital forms of remixing (Wilson, 2022). So, the fundamental unit—the basic building blocks of generative AI—is different from that of remix. And this difference may make a difference when it comes to addressing the ethical and legal challenges of this new kind of computational creativity.

7

THE FUTURE OF COMMUNICATION

Anytime you bring two seemingly different things into contact, like AI and communication, it is important to ask not only what AI means for communication but also what communication means for AI. We've already touched on some of this in the introduction, but here at the end, I want to take this further. Thus, the final chapter will propose and develop two complementary lines of thought: (1) the future of communication is AI, and (2) the future of AI is communication.

The former might appear to be rather self-evident as we have just laid out in detail various AI applications that are affecting the theory and practice of communication. But there is still something to this that needs to be further developed and formulated. The latter might be less evident—at least initially—but it will turn out to be no less important, as there are existing problems with AI that communication is well suited to resolve. After we sort this out, the final section of the chapter will conclude the book but looking at future ethical questions that confront us in the face of this confluence of communication and AI.

7.1 AI IS THE FUTURE OF COMMUNICATION

In 1950, the MIT computer scientist and progenitor of the new science of cybernetics Norbert Wiener made the following prediction:

DOI: 10.1201/9781003442240-7

Society can only be understood through a study of the messages
and the communication facilities which belong to it; and that in
the future development of these messages and communication
facilities, messages between man [SIC] and machines, between
machines and man, and between machine and machine, are
destined to play an ever-increasing part.

(Wiener, 1988, 16)

We now live in that world Wiener had envisioned, as machines of
all kinds participate in and are in the process of transforming both
communication and human social interaction.

7.1.1   COMMUNICATION AND TECHNOLOGY

Human communication and social organization have been dependent
on technology from ancient times. Writing, for instance, is credited
not only with the rise of cities and the development of laws and stable
political systems but also with the capability to record and preserve
innovations in both scientific inquiry and the practical arts. At the
time of its introduction, however, this was not a widely accepted
fact. Socrates—the big thought influencer of Athens—had been very
suspicious of this disruptive technology, going so far as to suggest
that it might destroy Greek civilization. But that clearly didn't happen.
In fact, it had the opposite effect. We only know about Socrates and
what he thought about writing, because Plato (1982) wrote it down
in a dialogue called the *Phaedrus* that we can still access and read today.

When it comes to these information and communication technologies, whether it is writing or any subsequent innovation, we
typically understand and make sense of it by situating it in the position of "medium" on the standard process model of communication.
According to this theoretical model, communication can be defined
as a dyadic process bounded, on the one side, by an information
source or sender and, on the other side, by a receiver. These two
participants are connected by a communication channel or medium
through which messages selected by the sender are conveyed to the

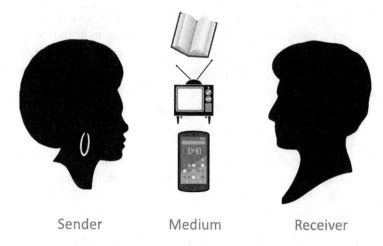

Sender   Medium   Receiver

FIGURE 7.1 Humans are the communicators and technologies are the medium.

receiver. In this transaction the two participants—the senders and receivers—are human subjects. The position of medium is occupied by various technological devices and systems. As Andrea Guzman (2018, 8) accurately describes it, "humans are communicators (senders and receivers) and technology is the medium, or channel, through which people exchange messages. This has been the dominant paradigm for communication research" (Figure 7.1).

7.1.2 COMPUTER-MEDIATED COMMUNICATION

Because this has been the dominant paradigm for thinking about the role and function of technology in human communication, it also applies to recent innovations, like the computer and the Internet. In fact, the last big innovation in the field of communication is arguable what is now called "computer-mediated communication" (CMC). CMC began to gain traction in the 1990s as the Internet disrupted and transformed all aspects of communication: email and SMS texting altered the form and function of interpersonal interactions, web content upended journalism and the newspaper industry, streaming media challenged the dominance of broadcast networks and existing models in mass communication, and social media has had a transformative impact on group and organizational communication.

CMC successfully locates the computer in the intermediate position of channel or medium. As such, it occupies the place of other forms of communication technology (e.g., print, telephone, radio, and television) and is comprehended as something through which human messages pass. This way of thinking has obviously worked well, and it has been successful, mainly because CMC successfully fit the potentially disruptive technology of the computer and Internet to the existing process model of communication.

7.1.3 FROM CMC TO AI-MC AND HMC

CMC has understandably become the dominant paradigm for understanding the role and function of the computer in communication. And its success is clearly evident by the institutionalization of CMC in professional organizations, university curricula, and standard textbooks and scholarly journals. But all of that might be over, precisely because of AI. As we have seen in the previous chapters, AI is not just a medium through which human messages pass from a human sender to human receivers; AI now occupies the place of sender and/or receiver in many communicative interactions.

We use MT applications that do more than transfer messages from human sender to receiver by changing the message itself and playing the role of interpreter. We talk directly to chatbots, and they respond to us in ways that makes it seem like they really understand what has been said. We connect with social robots, treating them not as some tool or instrument but as another socially significant other. And we ask (or prompt) generative AI applications to create an original story, image, or piece of music, and the algorithm not only follows our directions but can even explain what it did and why.

When the usual way of thinking about and making sense of things is challenged or put in question, there are generally two ways of formulating a response, which the Slovenian philosopher and cultural theorist Slavoj Žižek (2008, vii) has called "Ptolemization" and "Copernican revolution." The term "Ptolemization" indicates efforts to revise an existing framework or way of thinking by introducing increasingly complicated modifications and reconfigurations in an effort to ensure the continued functioning and success of the prevailing model.

"Copernican revolution," by contrast, designates not minor adjustments or revisions in the existing way of thinking but a complete reconfiguration or transformation of the accepted framework. The name, of course, comes from the Polish astronomer Nicolaus Copernicus, whose heliocentric model of the solar system provides the prototype for scientific revolution, insofar as it not only introduced a new framework but literally inverted or overturned the Ptolemaic system by moving the sun, which had been located on the periphery, to the center of the system.

The opportunities and challenges of AI are of this magnitude. The questions we now have to contend with are these: Can innovations in AI be accommodated to the usual way of thinking? Can they be Ptolemized and brought into accord with the existing CMC model? Or do these things disrupt that model and require revolutionary new frameworks, approaches, and research methods? Are we, in other words, in the midst or on the verge of what will be recognized as a Copernican revolution in communication? At this juncture—at this moment in history when the opportunities and challenges of AI for communication are first becoming identified, recognized, and addressed—there is evidence of both.

Efforts at Ptolemization have been advanced under the banner of "AI-Mediated Communication" (AI-MC). According to Hancock et al. (2020, 90), who first introduced the term, AI-MC can be defined as "mediated communication between people in which a computational agent operates on behalf of a communicator by modifying, augmenting, or generating messages to accomplish communication or interpersonal goals." A prime example of AI-MC is MT. With the current set of algorithmically controlled translation applications, the goal is to develop an intelligent—or at least a smart—intermediary, which can take the message of a human sender and modify or transform it into something that can be understood by the receiver. In MT, the sender and receiver remain human, but the intermediary does more than just transfer the message from the one to the other. It is a computational agent that modifies the message to accomplish a particular communication or interpersonal goal.

Human-machine communication (HMC), by contrast, pursues Copernican revolution, overturning the CMC framework and changing the rules of the game. The idea, which had been taking shape for a number of decades, was initially formalized in 2015 by Andrea Guzman and David J. Gunkel from Northern Illinois University and Steve Jones of the University of Illinois-Chicago. Unlike AI-MC, HMC recognizes that AI is not just a medium through which human messages pass but is itself another kind of communicative subject with whom one interacts. This shift, a shift that can be readily seen in the words that are used to describe it—from through to with and from what to whom—is not a modification or reworking of the existing CMC framework. It is a fundamental alteration in the subject of communication—understood as both the subject matter of communication and the communicative subject—that not only challenges existing ways of thinking about who or what communicates but opens up the opportunity for asking different kinds of questions and pursuing other ways of thinking about human beings, technology, and communication.

7.2 COMMUNICATION IS THE FUTURE OF AI

If we only focus our attention on the ways that AI is changing communication, we are only seeing part of the story. Communication can also alter how we understand and make sense of AI. In fact, "artificial intelligence" may itself already be a problem—a problem that communication can fix. Right now, AI is going through something of an identity crisis, as leading voices in the field are beginning to ask whether the name is (and maybe already was) a misnomer and a significant obstacle to accurate understanding. "As a computer scientist," Jaron Lanier (2023) wrote in a piece for *The New Yorker*, "I don't like the term A.I. In fact, I think it's misleading—maybe even a little dangerous."

7.2.1 *THE NAME GAME*

As we have already seen, what the term "artificial intelligence" designates has always been a bit murky and contentious. "AI people," as Roger Schank famously wrote in 1990,

> are fond of talking about intelligent machines, but when it comes down to it, there is little agreement on exactly what constitutes intelligence. And, it thus follows, there is very little agreement in AI about exactly what AI is and what it should be.

Because .there has been little agreement—even among experts in the field—about what AI is (or is not, for that matter), expectations for the technology are virtually unrestrained and prone to both overinflated hyperbole and doomerist predictions of the end of human civilization. As a result, we have been and continue to be involved with discussing and debating all kinds of speculative questions like: Can machines think? Are large language models sentient? Or when might we have an AI that achieves consciousness? For many researchers, scholars, and developers, however, these are not just the wrong questions, they are potentially dangerous lines of inquiry, because they suck up all the attention, distract us with dramatic speculative matters that are more science fiction than science fact, and therefore have the potential to cause us to miss many of the real harms of these technological systems and implementations.

7.2.2 BACK TO THE FUTURE

Since the difficulty derives from the very name "artificial intelligence," one solution has been to select or fabricate better or more accurate monikers. And the good news is that we do not have to look far or wide to find a viable alternative, as there was one already available at the time of the Dartmouth meeting with "cybernetics." This term—derived from the ancient Greek word κυβερνήτης for the helmsman of a boat—had been introduced and developed by Norbert Wiener in 1948 to designate the general science of communication and control in the animal and machine (Wiener, 1996). Cybernetics has at least three advantages when it comes to rebranding and updating what had been called AI.

First, it focuses attention on decision-making processes and control mechanisms. It does not get diverted by and lost in speculation about machine intelligence, which unfortunately directs attention to all kinds of cognitive capabilities, like consciousness, sentience, reason, understanding, as well as elaborate parlor games that have been used to test for their presence. Cybernetics is, by comparison, more modest. It is only concerned with communication signals and the effect they have on controlling decision-making outcomes. The principal example that has been utilized throughout the literature on the subject is the seemingly mundane thermostat. This homeostatic device can accurately adjust for temperature without knowing anything about the concept, understanding the difference between hot and cold, or needing to think or be thought to be thinking.

Second, and following from this, cybernetics avoids one of the main epistemological problems and sticking point that continually frustrates AI—"the problem of other minds." For McCarthy and colleagues, one of the objectives of the Dartmouth meeting—in fact, the first goal listed on the proposal—was to figure out "how to make machines use language." This is because language use—as Turing already had operationalized with the imitation game—had been taken to be a sign of intelligence. But as both chatbots and LLMs demonstrate, the manipulation of linguistic tokens can transpire without the algorithm knowing anything at all about the words it generates. Unlike AI, cybernetics can attend to the phenomenon and effect of this communicative behavior without needing to resolve or even broach the question concerning the problem of other minds or the issue of intelligence.

Finally, cybernetics does not make the same commitment to human exceptionalism that has been present in AI from the beginning. Because the objectives initially listed by the Dartmouth proposal (e.g., language use, form abstractions and concepts, solve problems reserved for humans, and improve themselves), definitions of AI tend to concentrate on the emulation or simulation of "human intelligence." Cybernetics by contrast is more diverse and less anthropocentric. As the general science of communication and control in the animal and the machine, it takes a more holistic view that can accommodate a wider range of things. It is, as N. Katherine Hayles (1999) argues, a posthuman framework that is able to respond to and take responsibility for others and other forms of socially significant otherness.

If this is the case and cybernetics already provided a viable alternative that could have helped us avoid many of the difficulties and blind alleys now associated with the term AI, one has to ask why "artificial intelligence" became the privileged designation in the first place? And there's a story here. As McCarthy (1996, 73) explained many years later, one of the reasons "for inventing the term 'artificial intelligence' was to escape association with cybernetics" and to "avoid having either to accept Norbert Wiener as a guru or having to argue with him." Thus, the term "artificial intelligence" was as much a political decision and strategy as it was a matter of scientific designation. But for this very reason, it is entirely possible and perhaps even prudent to reverse course and face what the nascent discipline of AI had so assiduously sought to avoid. The way forward may be by going back and reformulating AI as a communication science.

7.3 OPPORTUNITIES AND CHALLENGES

As technological artifacts of various configurations and capabilities come to occupy the position of another communicative and/or social subject, there are ethical questions—two in particular. At what point (if ever) can or should a robot, an algorithm, or other autonomous system be held responsible for the decisions it makes or the actions it deploys? When, in other words, would it make sense to say "It's the computer's fault?" Likewise, at what point (if ever) might we have to consider extending something like rights—civil, moral, or legal standing—to these socially active devices? When or how would something like "robot rights" be seen as necessary, useful, or both? This last section will not provide definitive answers to these queries but will instead investigate how and why these questions are important.

7.3.1 RESPONSIBILITY

One potential problem with technologies that appear to be another kind of communicative subject is that it will be increasingly difficult to decide who or what is doing the talking and can therefore be responsible for what is said or done. The way we usually sort this out is by relying on the instrumental theory of technology. According to this way of thinking, the machine—a computer, an NLP digital assistant, a social robot, etc.—can never be an end in and of itself; it is always a means, medium, or an instrument employed by human users for the purpose of humanly defined ends and objectives.

This way of thinking makes sense and is considered just good "common sense." Holding an AI application or robotic system accountable would be not only illogical but also irresponsible. This is because ascribing responsibility to machines could allow human subjects to blame computers for their mistakes. This is precisely what occurred early in 2024 with a chatbot that was used by Air Canada to handle customer service inquiries. In this case, a customer named Jake Moffatt contacted the airline to alter his flight plans due to a death in the family. The chatbot that handled Moffatt's request gave him incorrect information, advising him to book a new flight and then request a refund within 90 days. Moffatt did exactly as the chatbot advised, only to find that the airline would not honor the refund request. Moffatt pushed back, eventually taking his complaint to Canada's Civil Resolution Tribunal. In response to this filing, Air Canada argued the company should not be liable for the chatbot's misleading information because "the chatbot is a separate legal entity that is responsible for its own actions" (Yagoda, 2024). The judge was not persuaded and ruled—basically following the stipulations of the instrumentalist way of thinking—that Air Canada is liable for what its chatbot advised.

But this instrumentalist way of thinking, for all its notable success handling different kinds of technology, appears to be increasingly unable to contend with developments involving AI systems and applications, specifically those that have been designed using some form of machine learning. Consider, for example, Microsoft's Tay chatbot. Unlike many other chatbots, Tay did not simply follow prescribed instructions provided by its programmers but developed its conversational behaviors by exploiting discoverable patterns in existing data and from its own interactions with human users on social media platforms. And, as you might expect, Tay "learned" some bad and rather reprehensible behaviors, becoming a raving Neo-Nazi racist in just over 6 hours of operation.

When one asks the question: Who is responsible for Tay's bigoted comments? The answer is complicated. According to the standard instrumentalist way of thinking, one would need to blame the programmers at Microsoft, who designed the application to be able to do these things. But the programmers obviously did not set out to create a racist chatbot. So how did Microsoft answer for this? How did they explain and respond to the question concerning responsibility?

Initially a company spokesperson—in damage control mode—sent out an email to *Wired*, *The Washington Post*, and other news organizations that sought to blame the victim. According to this statement, it was not the programmers nor the corporation that could be held responsible for the hate speech. It's the fault of the users (or some users) who interacted with Tay and taught her to be a bigot. Tay's racism, in other word, is our fault. This is something that anyone familiar with crisis communication will tell you is an almost perfect example of what not to do.

Later, on Friday the 25th of March, Peter Lee, VP of Microsoft Research, posted the following apology on the Official Microsoft Blog:

> As many of you know by now, on Wednesday we launched a chatbot called Tay. We are deeply sorry for the unintended offensive and hurtful tweets from Tay, which do not represent who we are or what we stand for, nor how we designed Tay. Tay is now offline and we'll look to bring Tay back only when we are confident we can better anticipate malicious intent that conflicts with our principles and values.
>
> (Lee, 2016)

But this apology is also frustratingly unsatisfying or interesting (it all depends on how you look at it). According to Lee's carefully worded explanation, Microsoft is only responsible for not anticipating the bad outcome; it does not take responsibility or answer for the offensive material. For Lee, it is Tay who (or "that," and words matter here) is named and recognized as the source of the wildly inappropriate and reprehensible words and images. And since Tay is a kind of minor (a teenage chatbot) under the protection of her parent corporation, Microsoft needed to step in, apologize for their daughter's bad behavior, and put Tay in a time out.

Although the extent to which one may be prepared to assign agency and responsibility to these AI applications remains a contested matter, what is not debated is the fact that the rules of the game appear to be in flux and that there is evidence of a widening responsibility gap. In other words, the instrumental definition of technology, which had effectively tethered machine action to human agency and responsibility, no longer adequately applies to technologies that have been deliberately designed to operate and exhibit some form, no matter how rudimentary, of independent action or autonomous decision-making.

Consequently, we now have technologies that are designed to do things that deliberately exceed our control and ability to respond for what they do (or do not do). But let's be clear as to what this means. What is being argued is not that a chatbot, like Tay, is or should be considered a moral/legal subject and held solely accountable for the decisions it makes or the actions it deploys. That may be going too far. But what this does indicate is that AI systems, like Tay and many of the other applications we have discussed throughout this book, introduce significant complications into the standard way of assigning and dealing with responsibility. These AI systems and robotic devices might not be active agents in their own right (not yet at least), but the manner by which we conceptualize their operations and the way that they are designed to function effectively challenge the standard instrumentalist theory and open up fissures in the methods by which responsibility is typically decided, assigned, and formulated.

7.3.2 RIGHTS

The flipside to responsibility are rights. Typically, those individuals who we recognize as having social responsibilities also have rights that we are responsible for respecting and/or protecting. So, you can already see where this is going: If AI, robots, and other socially interactive systems can be said to have responsibilities, does that then mean they also deserve or should have rights? Or, if using that word in this context is too troubling, then at least some form of social standing and respect?

Before we can even begin to wrap our heads around this question, we should at least put in some effort to get rights right. If we don't, we might risk making the mistake that has derailed many journalists and aspiring critics, who have unfortunately assumed that even talking about this subject must mean and can only mean that we are talking about human rights for AI. But we aren't, as doing so would be both absurd and pointless. So let's take in three steps.

First, although we often use the word in everyday conversation, many of us do not know what rights, as both a moral and legal concept, actually entail. And we shouldn't feel bad about this. One hundred years ago, the American jurist Wesley Hohfeld (1920) observed that even experienced legal professionals tend to misunderstand the word. In order to address this problem, Hohfeld created a typology that breaks rights down into four related aspects or incidents: claims, powers, privileges, and immunities. His point was simple: A right, like the right one has to a piece of property, like a toaster or a computer, can be defined and characterized by one or more of these elements. It can, for instance, be formulated as a claim that the owner has over and against another individual. Or it could be expressed as an exclusive privilege for use and possession that is granted to the owner. Or it could be a combination of the two.

Second, the set of all possible rights for one category of entity, like an animal or an AI, is not necessarily equivalent to nor the same as that enjoyed by another category of entity, like a human being. One could, for instance, advance the proposal—introduced by the French legal team of Alain and Jérémy Bensoussan (2015)— that domestic social robots and SDS applications, like Siri or Alexa, have a right to privacy for the purposes of protecting the family's personal data. But considering this one right—the claim to privacy or the immunity from disclosure—does not and certainly should not mean that we also need to give it the vote.

Finally, and perhaps most importantly, there is a crucial difference between natural and legal rights. Natural rights are grounded in and derived from the essence or nature of the rights holder. Human rights, for instance, are anchored in and justified by "human nature." In many religious traditions, for instance, this is something that is typically explained and justified by appeal to divine or transcendental authority. In Christianity, for instance, the "rights of man" (and the gender-exclusive construction is an unfortunate aspect of this formulation) are justified by the doctrine of the *imago dei*, the belief that human beings have been created in the image of God and bestowed by their creator with inalienable rights. In non-religious or secular traditions, the determining factors are, as Leif Wenar (2020) explains in his article for the *Stanford Encyclopedia of Philosophy*, often "the same sorts of attributes described in more or less metaphysical or moralized terms: free will, rationality, autonomy, or the ability to regulate one's life in accordance with one's chosen conception of the good life."

Legal rights, by contrast, are rights that exist under the rules of a specific legal system and are decided and justified by human authorities. This is both good and bad news. First the good news. Unlike natural rights, legal rights do not need to engage in fanciful metaphysical speculations about the essential nature of things nor appeal to supernatural authorities, the existence of which can always be doubted or questioned. But—and here's the bad news—that means that legal rights are a matter of human decision-making and that the assignment, distribution, and protection of these rights are ultimately a matter of finite exercises of terrestrial power. Where natural rights are anchored in eternal metaphysical truths that can be discussed and debated by theologians and philosophers, legal rights are legitimated by earthy exercises of specific socio-political power.

At this point in time, it seems very unlikely that AI or robots would have access to or the need for natural rights or their protections. As human designed and built technologies, these devices do not have nor do they seem to be on the cusp of possessing any of the qualifying natural properties or capabilities to be the subject of natural rights. But legal rights are another matter altogether. All that is necessary for an AI or robot to have a specific legal right is that someone in the position of power—a legislative body or a judge—decides that the artifact deserves some level of social status and protection. And if we look at things from that perspective, robots already have rights.

In November 2020, the General Assembly of Pennsylvania passed Act 106 that classifies autonomous delivery robots, or what the text of the act calls "personal delivery devices" (PDD), as pedestrians in order to provide a legal framework for their deployment on city streets and sidewalks (Pennsylvania General Assembly, 2020). Similar laws have been passed in a number of other jurisdictions, including the Commonwealth of Virginia (2021), which provides the following stipulation: "a personal delivery device operating on a sidewalk or crosswalk shall have all the rights and responsibilities applicable to a pedestrian under the same circumstance." In granting these limited rights and responsibilities to personal delivery robots, the State Legislature was not seeking to revolve or even address the big questions of robot moral standing or AI and robot personhood. It was simply seeking to provide a legal framework for the integration of the robot into existing legal practices and to align those with evolving social needs.

The alliterative phrase "robot rights" might sound like something out of science fiction, but asking about the rights of AI and robots—especially their legal rights—is important for us right here and right now. Rights are simply one of the tools we already have at our disposal for integrating things into our existing social, moral, and legal structures. The AI and robots might not care one way or the other—and they most likely are indifferent about it at best—but we care. That means that asking about and entertaining responses to the question of robot rights is not about the artifacts. It is about us and the integrity of our moral and legal institutions. It is about how we—individually and together—decide to organize our social environment in the face of socially disruptive technologies like AI and robots.

REFERENCES

AI 100 (2016). *One Hundred Year Study on Artificial Intelligence*. Stanford: Stanford University. https://ai100.stanford.edu/sites/default/files/ai100report10032016fnl_singles.pdf

Barthes, Roland (1978). Death of the author. In *Image, Music, Text*, Trans. Stephen Heath, 142–148. New York: Hill & Wang.

Baudrillard, Jean (1994). *Simulacra and Simulation*. Trans. S. F. Glaser. Ann Arbor: University of Michigan Press.

Bekey, George A. (2015). *Autonomous Robots: From Biological Inspiration to Implementation and Control*. Cambridge, MA: MIT Press.

Bensoussan, Alain and Jérémy Bensoussan (2015). *Droit des Robots* [The Law of Robots]. Brussels, BE: Éditions Larcier.

Bessi, Alessandro and Emilio Ferrara (2016). Social bots distort the 2016 U.S. Presidential election online discussion. *First Monday* 21(11). https://doi.org/10.5210/fm.v21i11.7090

Breazeal, Cynthia (2002). *Designing Sociable Robots*. Cambridge, MA: MIT Press.

Breazeal, Cynthia (2003). Toward sociable robots. *Robotics and Autonomous Systems* 42(1): 167–175. https://doi.org/10.1016/S0921-8890(02)00373-1

Bubeck, Sébastien et al. (2023). Sparks of artificial general intelligence: Early experiments with GPT-4. *Arxiv Computer Science*. https://doi.org/10.48550/arXiv.2303.12712

Čapek, Karel (2009). R.U.R. (*Rossum's Universal Robots*), Trans. David Wyllie. Gloucestershire, UK: The Echo Library.

Carey, James W. (1989). *Communication as Culture: Essays on Media and Society*. New York: Routledge.

Cho, Kyunghyun, Bart van Merriënboer, Caglar Gulcehre, Fethi Bougares, Holger Schwenk, Dzmitry Bahdanau and Yoshua Bengio (2014). Learning Phrase Representations using RNN Encoder-Decoder for Statistical Machine Translation. *Proceedings of the 2014 Conference on Empirical Methods in Natural Language Processing (EMNLP)*: 1724–1734.

Churchland, Paul (1999). *Matter and Consciousness*. Cambridge, MA: MIT Press.

Commonwealth of Virginia (2021). Personal delivery vehicles. *Virginia Code* § 46.2–908.1:1. https://law.lis.virginia.gov/vacode/title46.2/chapter8/section46.2-908.1:1/

Cope, David (2001). *Virtual Music: Computer Synthesis of Musical Style*. Cambridge, MA: MIT Press.

Cope, David (2017). *Experiments in Musical Intelligence (Website)*. http://artsites.ucsc.edu/faculty/cope/experiments.htm

Darling, Kate (2021). *The New Breed: What Our History with Animals Reveals about Our Future with Robots*. New York: Henry Holt and Company.

de Vries, Alex (2023). The growing energy footprint of artificial intelligence. *Joule* 7(10): p2191–p2194. https://doi.org/10.1016/j.joule.2023.09.004

Dewey, John (1916). *Democracy and Education*. New York: Macmillan.

Epstein, Robert (2007). From Russia, with love: How I got fooled (and Somewhat Humiliated) by a computer. *Scientific American Mind*. www.scientificamerican.com/article/from-russia-with-love/

Esposito, Roberto (2015). *Persons and Things*, Trans. Zakiya Hanafi. Cambridge, MA: Polity.

Ferguson, Kirby (2014). *Everything is a Remix (4 Part Video Series)*. http://everythingisaremix.info/

Guzman, Andrea L. (2018). *Human Machine Communication: Rethinking Communication, Technology and Ourselves*. New York: Peter Lang.

Hancock, Jeffrey T., Mor Naaman and Karen Levy (2020). AI-mediated communication: Definition, research agenda, and ethical considerations. *Journal of Computer-Mediated Communication* 25(1): 89–100. https://doi.org/10.1093/jcmc/zmz022

Hayles, Nancy Katherine (1999). *How We Became Posthuman: Virtual Bodies in Cybernetics, Literature, and Informatics*. Chicago, IL: University of Chicago Press.

Hohfeld, Wesley (1920). *Fundamental Legal Conceptions as Applied in Judicial Reasoning*. New Haven, CT: Yale University Press.

Jibo (2014). Promotional video. *YouTube*. www.youtube.com/watch?v= H0h20jRA5M0

Lanier, Jaron (2023). There is no A.I. *The New Yorker*. www.newyorker.com/science/annals-of-artificial-intelligence/there-is-no-ai

Lee, Peter (2016). Learning from Tay's introduction. *Official Microsoft Blog*, 25 March. https://blogs.microsoft.com/blog/2016/03/25/learning-tays-introduction/

McCarthy, John (1996). *Defending AI Research: A Collection of Essays and Reviews*. Stanford, CA: CSLI Publications.

McCarthy, John, Marvin L. Minsky, Nathan Rochester and Claude E. Shannon (1955). *A Proposal for the Dartmouth Summer Research Project on Artificial Intelligence*. http://jmc.stanford.edu/articles/dartmouth/dartmouth.pdf

McQuate, Sarah (2023). Q&A: UW researcher discusses just how much energy ChatGPT uses. *UW News*. www.washington.edu/news/2023/07/27/how-much-energy-does-chatgpt-use/

Mori, Masahiro (2012). The Uncanny Valley, Trans. Karl F. MacDorman and Norri Kageki. *IEEE Robotics & Automation Magazine* 19(2): 98–100. https://doi.org/10.1109/MRA.2012.2192811

Natale, Simone (2021). *Deceitful Media: Artificial Intelligence and Social Life after the Turing Test*. New York: Oxford University Press.

Navas, Eduardo (2012). *Remix Theory: The Aesthetics of Sampling*. Wien: Springer.

Nourbakhsh, Illah (2013). *Robot Futures*. Cambridge, MA: MIT Press.

Obvious (2018). *Obvious Art—Website*. http://obvious-art.com

Pennsylvania General Assembly (2020). *Vehicle Code (75 PA.C.S)–Personal Delivery Devices and Making Editorial Changes*. Act 106. https://www.legis.state.pa.us/cfdocs/legis/li/uconsCheck.cfm?yr=2020&sessInd=0&act=106

Peterson, Andrea (2013). On the internet, no one knows you're a bot. And that's a problem. *The Washington Post*, 13 August. www.washingtonpost.com/news/the-switch/wp/2013/08/13/on-the-internet-no-one-knows-youre-a-bot-and-thats-a-problem/?utm_term=.b4e0dd77428a

Plato (1982). *Plato I: Euthyphro, Apology, Crito, Phaedo, Phaedrus*, Trans. H. N. Fowler. Cambridge, MA: Harvard University Press.

Plato (1987). *Republic*. Trans. P. Shorey. Cambridge, MA: Harvard University Press.

Poibeau, Thierry (2017). *Machine Translation*. Cambridge, MA: MIT Press.

Reeves, Byron and Clifford Nass (1996). *The Media Equation: How People Treat Computers, Television, and New Media Like Real People and Places*. Cambridge, MA: Cambridge University Press.

Rollins, Henry (2007). *Henry Rollins On Rave and Modern Rock Music*. www.youtube. com/watch?v=AyRDDOpKaLM

Roose, Kevin (2022). AI-generated art won a prize. Artists aren't happy. *The New York Times*. www.nytimes.com/2022/09/02/technology/ai-artificial-intelligence-artists.html

Schank, Roger C. (1990). What is AI anyway? In *The Foundations of Artificial Intelligence: A Sourcebook*, eds. Derek Partridge and Yorick Wilks, 3–13. Cambridge, MA: Cambridge University Press.

Scheutz, Matthias (2012). The inherent dangers of unidirectional emotional bonds between humans and social robots. In *Robot Ethics: The Ethical and Social Implications of Robotics*, eds. Patrick Lin, Keith Abney and George A. Bekey, 205–221. Cambridge, MA: MIT Press.

Schrader, Adam (2023). Another A.I.-generated artwork was denied copyright protection, adding a new knot to the complexities of creative ownership. *ArtNet*. https://news.artnet.com/art-world/ai-art-copyright-2367590

Shannon, Claude E. and Warren Weaver (1949). *The Mathematical Theory of Communication*. Urbana, IL: University of Illinois Press.

SoftBank Robotics (2018). *Pepper*. www.softbankrobotics.com/emea/en/pepper.

Sokolowski, Robert (1988). Natural and artificial intelligence. *Daedalus* 117(1): 45–64.

Steiner, George (1975). *After Babel*. New York: Oxford University Press.

Sweeney, Miriam E. (2020). Digital assistants. In *Uncertain Archives: Critical Keywords for Big Data*, eds. N. B. Thylstrup, D. Agostinho, A. Ring, C. D'Ignazio and K. Veel. Cambridge, MA: MIT Press.

Tabini, Marco (2013). Inside Siri's brain: The challenges of extending Apple's virtual assistant. *MacWorld*, 8 April. www.macworld.com/article/2033073/inside-siris-brain-the-challenges-of-extending-apples-virtual-assistant.html.

Tangermann, Victor (2024). Sam Altman says AI using too much energy, will require breakthrough energy source. *Futurism*, 17 January. https://futurism.com/sam-altman-energy-breakthrough

The New York Times Company v. Microsoft Corporation (2024) 1:23-cv-11195, (S.D.N.Y.)

Turing, Alan (1999). Computing machinery and intelligence. In *Computer Media and Communication: A Reader*, ed. Paul A. Meyer, 37–58. Oxford: Oxford University Press.

Turkle, Sherry (2011). *Alone Together: Why We Expect More from Technology and Less from Each Other*. New York: Basic Books.

Weaver, Warren (1949). Translation. *The Rockefeller Foundation.* www.mt-archive. info/Weaver-1949.pdf

Weizenbaum, Joseph (1967). Contextual understanding by computers. *Communications of the ACM* 10(8): 474–480. https://doi.org/10.1145/363534.363545

Weizenbaum, Joseph (1976). *Computer Power and Human Reason: From Judgment to Calculation.* San Francisco, CA: W. H. Freeman.

Wenar, Leif (2020). Rights. In *The Stanford Encyclopedia of Philosophy,* ed. Edward N. Zalta, Spring 2021 Edition. https://plato.stanford.edu/archives/spr2021/ entries/rights/.

Wiener, Norbert (1988). *The Human Use of Human Beings: Cybernetics and Society,* Boston, MA: Da Capo Press.

Wiener, Norbert (1996). *Cybernetics: Or Control and Communication in the Animal and the Machine.* Cambridge, MA: MIT Press.

Wikipedia (2024). *Deepfake.* https://en.wikipedia.org/wiki/Deepfake

Wilson, Scott (2022). Interview: Holly Herndon & Mat Dryhurst. *Fact Magazine.* www.factmag.com/2023/05/25/holly-herndon-mat-dryhurst-interview/

Yagoda, Maria (2024). Airline held liable for its chatbot giving passenger bad advice—What this means for travellers. *BBC.* https://www.bbc.com/travel/ article/20240222-air-canada-chatbot-misinformation-what-travellers- should-know

Žižek, Slavoj (2008). *The Sublime Object of Ideology.* London: Verso.

Zuboff, Shoshana (2019). *The Age of Surveillance Capitalism: The Fight for a Human Future at the New Frontier of Power.* London: Profile Books.

Printed in the United States
by Baker & Taylor Publisher Services